PODCASTS SUCK!
(if you don't have one)

A Step By Step Guide To Launching Your Podcast

By Sebastian Rusk

Foreword by: Brittany Krystal

ISBN: 978-0-578-75766-7

Table of Contents

Foreword

When Sebastian reached out to me to write the foreword for this book on podcasting, it was an immediate "hell yes!" from me.

Why? Not only is the power of podcasting *very* real, but Sebastian also had a hand in helping me get started on my podcast journey.

Starting the Beyond Influential Podcast has easily been one of the most transformational decisions I've made that not only changed the trajectory of my business, but also my life. I didn't know at the time just how big of an impact it was going to have. I was excited to have valuable conversations with those I wanted to learn from, but I couldn't have predicted the doors it would open or the relationships it would help me establish and build.

As a personal branding and growth expert, I knew about the power of building personal brand and content creation before I started my podcast. I had seen first-hand the results as I had worked behind the scenes for some of the heaviest hitters online, including Gary Vaynerchuk, Marie Forleo & Tom Bilyeu to grow their brands and businesses. I saw what was possible through personal branding and knew you didn't need some special "it" factor to do it successfully, but I also recognized that you *do* need to be creating some form of content consistently. For me, that was through podcasting.

Podcasting appealed to me because I didn't have to make it a huge production with hair and makeup or put a ton of pressure on myself to make it perfect. Instead, I could focus on having a quality conversation. Substance over the superficial. It was also content I owned that wasn't specific to one particular social media platform, which is always an additional bonus. I had the idea for Beyond Influential in 2016, a year before I actually launched, when I was still working on Team Garyvee at VaynerMedia. Why didn't I start sooner? Honestly, I wish I had. But I will say this, as soon as I made the commitment to start the podcast, Sebastian was the first person I approached to see if he had any recommendations for editors, and not surprisingly, he delivered. Sebastian introduced me to my podcast editor, who has been working with me since day 1 of the Beyond Influential podcast.

So, how did I meet Sebastian?

He popped out from behind a large potted plant at a hotel. Literally. (And it still cracks me up every time I think about it.)

I met Sebastian in March 2017 when he was MC-ing at Digital Marketer's Traffic & Conversion Summit. I was there to produce content for a client who was a keynote speaker at the event. As I was waiting for my client, and as I was used to working behind the scenes, I wasn't expecting anyone to "recognize" me. Sebastian's surprise appearance startled me and on top of that, he knew my name from seeing me on Garyvee's content. And we've built our relationship since!

This much about Sebastian was immediately obvious: whether he's MCing an event, working with a client, or anything else he undertakes, he pursues it relentlessly, energetically, and enthusiastically. Not only that, he does it from a place of true service. He is passionate about helping you start a podcast, and giving you the tools to do it successfully.

He is now several years deep into helping others launch their podcast through his PodcastLaunchLab.com program, and this book contains the knowledge and tips he's picked up along the way.

If you're on the fence at all about podcasting, it's time to get off of it because you won't regret starting one.

Podcasting can change your life and this book can help you get started.

xx,

Brittany

Thinking About Launching a Podcast For Your Brand?

If so, I'd like to start this book by telling you that ANYTHING is possible and YES YOU CAN!

You can launch a successful podcast for your brand and become a media company, regardless of your profession (plumber, doctor, lawyer, etc.).

If you want to avoid newbie mistakes and truly learn how to successfully launch a podcast for your business, you picked up the right book, keep reading.

Back in 2013, I launched my first online radio show via BlogTalkRadio. That platform worked for some time but having to do the show live every day became very time-consuming. At times, the BlogTalkRadio platform would fail me miserably; in times of need and usually when I had a popular guest on.

It was then I learned you should never depend on new technology when creating consistent, valuable content, because things change, and, like me, you could be left holding the bag.

After a two-and-a-half-year hiatus, new technology came on the scene. It was THE DEAL: it was called Blab. It was awesome because it allowed you to host a "LIVE" video show via Livestream and have guests join you in different video chat windows for what was an all-around highly engaging experience. Well, that was until Blab became obsolete. Once again, I found myself out of the podcast space due to the failure of some company I had nothing to do with. I learned right then and there not to depend on software(s) I couldn't control and people I didn't know to dictate my success with a podcast.

Late in 2019, I decided I was going to relaunch my show for the third time. This time, I was going to control the entire process from A-Z.

Was this a lot of work to conceptualize, record, produce, edit, post, and promote each episode? ABSOLUTELY! But this time around, I knew it was going to help contribute to providing valuable content to my community.

The coolest part about this: the show ended up being so good, and people were so fired up about the quality of my podcast, they began asking me how to set up a podcast for their own business.

As I continued to field these questions, it became very clear to me there was a huge gap in the market. I quickly realized my podcast journey thus far held the keys to unlocking a valuable podcast solution for brands and marketers to capitalize on. Becoming a media company and producing a podcast show for their brand allows them to become an authority in their space.

This, my friends, is when I sat down and mapped the core steps it takes to launch your very own podcast show.

Download the **"TOP 5 REASONS YOUR BRAND NEEDS A PODCAST"** here: **PodcastLaunchLab.com**

Chapter 1
My Journey into Podcasting

How I Started

Maybe it was the fact that I grew up in a radio station watching my father as a DJ that made podcasting come so naturally. I had a premonition podcasting would disrupt (and eventually replace) traditional radio as we know it. I was all for it, too! I mean, when is the last time you hopped in your car or turned on a radio and were eager to listen to yet another DJ talk over your favorite song? I assume your answer is, "never."

We didn't know it yet (or maybe some did) back in 2008, but we were entering an "audio era" with technology. With voice recognition being around and technology like the Amazon Alexa arriving, speaking things into existence is now a reality.

I decided to start a podcast right out of the gate when I launched my brand, SocialBuzzTV.com. My thought about podcasting was, "Why not?" I'd discovered an online platform called BlogTalkRadio an online radio station. Easy to share, my guests would call into a phone number, I could record the episode and BlogTalkRadio helped me get my show into iTunes. Needless to say, I was STOKED!

The only problem was - the technology of BlogTalkRadio was NEW, and with NEW comes problems and challenges.

Why I Quit Three Times

Starting is easy; sticking with it, not so much.

It's always fun and games when you first start a podcast. Then you get ten episodes in and start questioning your motives. The biggest challenge when starting a podcast is. . . sticking to it.

Statistics will tell us the average podcast doesn't make it past six episodes. I must mention this early in this book so you understand the commitment. Continuing to stay consistent with recording new episodes and publishing new content is the lifeline keeping your podcast out of the graveyard.

A creative way I found to keep myself accountable for creating new content is to enroll people within my network into the process. I tease future episodes that are coming out with notable guests that people may have an interest in. Now, the reality is, if I don't follow through with what I'm talking about to my network, there probably aren't any consequences, other than those that I've put on myself to remain accountable. More times than not, accountability will keep us in our place, especially when it comes to creating content. In the beginning, when you're first starting a podcast, there is no immediate monetizing or big reason (other than your "Why I'm starting a podcast") that is going to keep you consistent with continually recording new episodes and creating new content.

When I first started my podcast, I knew that it was going to be the future, eventually. Little did I know I would end up podcasting full-time six years later. My original show started in 2011 on BlogTalkRadio. This platform sold me on the idea of creating my online radio show with their platform. The only challenge I had by utilizing this platform, was when they had technical difficulties, then it became my problem. For example, if I had a guest scheduled for my show and it had taken me a lot of time to get this guest scheduled, and their platform went belly-up for whatever technical reason. This problem caused me to stop recording my shows on BlogTalkRadio.

Shortly after stopping my show on BlogTalkRadio, I was offered an opportunity to have a radio show on a local AM radio station in Miami, Florida. All of this was new to me, so of course I was excited and immediately said, "Yes." The radio station happened to need some help with their social media efforts *(as did everyone back in 2011)*, so they were willing to do a swap with me and give me airtime in exchange for me promoting their radio station, as well as helping them with their social media strategy.

It was an everyday thing to get excited about. Another venture bringing me a step closer to wherever it was I was going. A radio show? Sounds exciting. This was going to build some real credibility into my resume. Once again, it was the beginning, and I was all excited. So, eagerly, every Friday at 4:30, I would wade through Miami traffic to get to a radio station that had wooden walls and looked like it hadn't been updated since 1971. Moreover, the management team wasn't exactly what I expected.

One day, I was approached by one of the station managers, and they told me I needed to talk about the radio station more and not about my brand or my show, but the radio station. I stood there and I stared at the guy like he had ten heads and boogers. I mean, I was willing to trade my time in exchange for a radio show on an AM radio station. Eventually, I got fed up, and I pulled the show. I told the guy to go talk about his radio station, I was out of there. Some would call it insubordinate; I call it smart. It makes zero sense to me to answer to somebody who did not get it that the station was in an industry that was quickly being replaced by podcasting.

Leaving the station was a move that I'll never regret; it allowed me to reignite my excitement for podcasting. I decided to relaunch my show for the second time. This time, I wouldn't record every single day. I would do something once a week. Then I continually told myself a lie. "No one cares what I'm saying, no one cares about content, I shouldn't waste my time."

It's amazing how we make up these stories in our head, and we believe them, though they are not true.

So there I was, restarting my podcast for the second time. I still felt I needed to have a podcast somehow, someway, someday.

For the second time, I was without a podcast, and then the end of 2016 rolled around. In 2016, I met a friend who encouraged me to sign up for a personal development course that she was in called, "Gratitude Training."

I was extremely resistant toward it.

But in the back of my mind, I knew personal development was vital to success as an entrepreneur.

I joined the course and took two of the three parts of the program. It took me ninety days to get through it. I feel like I checked out of life for those three months while I took the course. I think that's how life works sometimes; it just goes on hold so you can focus on what needs to be done. Going internally and doing the work of personal development is a messy job; but someone has to do it, and that someone is only you.

Why do I bring this up? Because on the back of my taking that course and coming out of what I used to consider extreme heartbreak, I would start to become my brand.

Getting Serious About Podcasting

Let's get the hard stuff out of the way first.

Just like anything in life, anything worth doing is going to be hard. Not going to the gym and becoming overweight is hard and going to the gym and working out is hard. My buddy always said to me, "CHOOSE YOUR HARD."

Don't get me wrong, starting a podcast is not impossible, and it's not going to be the hardest work you've ever done in your life, but I don't want to downplay it by saying it's easy and doesn't require a ton of effort. The amount of effort you're putting into your podcast is entirely up to you. Like most things in life that require effort, you're going to get out of it what you put into it. The more you put into your show, the faster it's going to grow, the bigger your community gets, the more opportunities present themselves, and the faster you get to where you're able to monetize your show and make a business out of it.

You must commit to it and stick with it (read that again).

Anything worth doing is never an easy thing, but it's often worth it. Your commitment to starting a podcast is entirely up to you. The best part about having a podcast is that you remain in control. You decide how many times you're going to record your podcast every month. You decide what type of content you're going to produce.

I'm not here to tell you how committed you should be with anything in life, but as a fellow podcaster, I can tell you: with no commitment, there is no podcast.

Throughout this book, I'll continue to touch on commitment and how important it is in having a podcast or maintaining, restarting, and starting a podcast.

If you're going to do this, then do it. Commit to it, set some goals and become accountable by sharing with your community what you're doing.

Oh, and FYI, it isn't always "fun."

Yes, having a podcast can be very fun! Do not misunderstand me when I say it isn't always fun. When you're first getting started, if you are the one recording your show, editing your show, posting your show, marketing your show, and doing all of the work, you will most likely not consider all of that "fun."

As new shows grow, things will become more streamlined. You'll be able to farm things out; editing the podcast, having a virtual assistant, and having someone on your team to help you with the marketing of the show and each episode.

I've been able to outsource the tasks I used to do. I would consider that "FUN." Now I no longer have to do it because I have a system in place which allows me to streamline the process of producing my podcast. I only want to be able to focus on what I'm good at, which is creating new episodes and telling stories.

I must forewarn you: not every episode you record is going to be something you're anticipating. When you first start recording your series of episodes, it feels like quite a daunting task. Like most things that require effort, the story we're telling ourselves about that task could be the very thing that holds us back from actually completing the task.

Be careful with the story you're telling yourself before you start to record a podcast episode. Most likely, the story that you're telling yourself isn't even true. With that being said, be true to yourself and ask, "Is the story I'm telling myself true?" This isn't a book about personal development. This is a book about starting a podcast. But starting a podcast has a lot to do with life. . . which has a lot to do with developing as a human being in general. Hence, why I bring this up.

How do you get someone to do something? You create an opportunity that makes them want to do it. That same theory applies when creating leverage on yourself to get a task done; like recording a podcast episode. You have to make it fun, you've got to make it empowering, and you have to make it motivating. For yourself, this will ease the process or clear out anything holding you back from actually recording the podcast episode. Remember, we are far too inside our heads most times when attempting to complete even the simplest tasks. Once we get out of our own way, we find that it's extremely simple to complete the task if we make it fun for ourselves.

Be Ready for Resistance on Your End, Lean into it

Resistance is a phenomenal indicator you're on the right track and that you should be doing something. I heard a quote once that said, "What we resist, persists." I couldn't agree more. Have you ever ignored something but it doesn't just go away and you finally cave in and give attention to it only to realize you should have been doing this since you heard about it?

Resistance is extremely powerful; if you leverage it for yourself. Every time you feel resistant about moving forward in taking a step toward launching a podcast, just remember: resistance is yet another reminder you should be starting a podcast or taking up that hobby or taking that trip you've been putting off. Resistance is the best reminder of what we should be doing. When we start thinking like that, the power of resistance starts to show things through a different lens. Resistance is a tool. Resistance is something we can leverage to get done what we need to get done and get to where it is that we want to be.

Push Through it

Have you ever dreaded having to do something but when you finally did it, you looked at things completely differently? I think we've all been there once or twice before.

When I think of pushing through it, I think of it as a workout. There isn't a day that goes by that I wake up and say, "Wow, I really can't wait to get to the gym, do some exercises, lift some weights and run and jump and sweat!" I've never once told myself that. I do tell myself when I wake up every morning that it's time to work out: *The payoff is far greater than my resistance about wanting to go to the gym.* The payoff refers to the feeling that I have when I'm done working out. The feeling of accomplishment. The feeling of being healthy. The most important feeling of pushing through; pushing through my doubts, pushing through my resistance, and just getting it done.

Whatever is on the Other Side is Worth it

Let me encourage you for a minute by saying that this time next year you will be so glad you started your podcast. We often put things off for weeks, months, even years. Sometimes, things never even get done because of our putting off efforts. How much closer does that get us to where we want to be from where we currently are? Stay focused on what's on the other side of starting a podcast, versus everything involved with actually starting a podcast. The very fact you can record a podcast with an iPhone 6 with no professional equipment, just a quiet room and a smartphone, is mind-boggling in and of itself. Sit with that thought for a minute. The thought that if you start your podcast now, this time next year you will be so much further along than you could have ever expected.

When you get serious, your growth gets serious.

It's funny how things work out when we get serious about them. I can tell you from my own experience; the more serious I've been about a project, the more growth I've experienced while creating that project. Growth comes from getting serious about the things we are extremely passionate about and the things we want to do but we've been putting off. Things like starting a podcast.

Podcasting can be a hobby, but, usually, it's going to be an extension of your brand. That requires you to be serious about what you're doing. Not being serious when starting your podcast is just setting yourself up for disaster.

You Have to Build it, and Yes, They Will Come, WITH Effort From You

There's an old saying, "If you build it, they will come." With little or no effort, nothing is going to come to fruition. You have to build it. You have to build your show brick by brick, step by step, and grow your community along with it. As the show grows in your community, and with your continual, consistent effort, yes, your audience will show up.

No one cares in the beginning. You have to build trust and community at the same time.

Your first couple of episodes are probably not going to matter to people outside of your immediate circle.

That's just how it works when we start something new. It's your job to educate and motivate listeners, differentiate your show and create interest around it outside of your inner circle of friends and contacts and those you associate with daily. I'm talking about getting the word out and growing a community above and beyond people you're already connected to. That happens when you're creating valuable content that people consume. The people who talk about the shows, exchange ideas, and recommend your show to others.

Even though your community may not seem like it matters in the beginning because it's so small, it does matter to stay focused on what community you've served. As you continue to do that, they will support your efforts, recommend your efforts, and endorse your efforts.

I'm excited for you to start this journey of podcasting, and you should be too. I wrote this book not only to show you how to start a podcast, but to motivate you and empower you to start a podcast.

Use this book as a guide and a tool, but don't let that get in the way of your creativity when starting your podcast. The only goal I have is to see people start a podcast. Whether they read this book and hire me or don't hire me to help them start the podcast, I just want to see them get a podcast started.

Buckle your seatbelt! It's going to be a wild ride that's all going to be worth it! Let's get to work, future podcaster!

True grit

Google defines true grit as, "Noun (uncountable) spirit; courage; moral stamina."

I couldn't think of three better words to better describe what true grit is. Podcasting isn't for everyone. It is definitely for those who have spirit, courage, and moral stamina, just like the definition says. You have to be willing to continue and fight on, even when you don't want to, when it comes to being successful with podcasting.

Creativeness

Your creativeness will take you a long way with podcasting. Your ability to tell stories and strategically interview people with interesting stories will give you an advantage. While creativeness isn't required, it is highly recommended. Creativity is what keeps your audience engaged, it's what gets your audience to tell other people about your show, it's what gets your audience to support you, no matter what.

Consistency

Consistency is key.

I'll talk a lot about it in this book: mindset, procrastination, and being "all in" when starting a podcast. Consistency is the secret ingredient to being a long-term, successful podcaster. If you can remain consistent with keeping your word and continuing to record podcast episodes, that consistency is going to pay off in the long run. Think about anything you've been consistent with in your life. When you're consistent with it, you become better at it.

The desire to tell a story

If you don't have a desire to tell the story, people are not going to have a desire to listen to what you're talking about. Stories have to resonate with the audience. You have to have a strong desire and interest in telling your story in a very effective format. Podcasting makes it easy to do that, but you must have the will and desire to actually want to tell a story. Stories can't just be made up, unless, of course, your podcast is about some fictional topic that you find amusing; and so would your listeners.

Focused

Someone once told me the acronym for focus is, "Forever On Course Until Successful." I never forgot that. And every time I think of the word "focus," I think about that acronym. The only way to get to where we're going is to remain focused. We decide what our focus is going to be on. We can focus on not being productive, we can focus on business, we can focus on our family, we can focus on nothing, we can focus on things that are irrelevant. That's our decision to make.

I'm not going to tell you what to do, but I am telling you that you must be focused if you want to start a podcast. If you're not focused on the task at hand, it's never going to get done. Or maybe you will start, but you won't continue.

There's a tremendous amount of power that comes with being focused. When you're focused, you're motivated, you have a strong desire to win! When you're focused, nothing can get in your way. The blinders are on, and you're on a mission to accomplish what it is that you want to do. In this case, it's starting a podcast. Staying focused on figuring out what your podcast is going to be about; whom you're going to interview, what type of value you're going to bring to the world, and what the overall outcome and goal is in launching a podcast. If you focus on this process, it makes it easier to get to where you're going that much faster.

Open

I think the quote says, "I just wish that closed minds came with closed mouths."

There's a lot of truth in that statement. More often than not, the individuals who are the most critical are the most closed-minded individuals. I strongly encourage you to stay away from those people whilst embarking on your quest for a podcast.

Shoulda, Coulda, Woulda, JUST STOP!

How many times do you find yourself saying these words over and over and over again? It happens more times than not. I think sometimes we get stuck in a mindset where we just want to talk about what we should be doing as opposed to what we're actually doing. And then there's time for talking about what we can do instead of actually doing what we're supposed to do. And then there's some of us who live in the past and talk about what we would have done, which, by the way, no one cares about.

The only thing someone cares about is what you're doing right now. If you're doing something to serve other people, all the better. The fact that you're not in this game just for yourself will resonate with your audience.

If you take note of how many times you say you should have, would have, and could have done in your daily life, you'll find you're saying it more times than you realize. Speaking those three phrases is a form of living in the past. There is no mention of the present in those words of "shoulda, coulda, woulda." I guess you could say I should be doing this in the present moment, but in my mind, utilizing words like that is simply making excuses to procrastinate and keep yourself further from where you want to be.

When launching your podcast and continuing to produce your podcast, you must stay ready. It contributes to being open and everything I mentioned above. But even more than all those things, you need to be ready at all times: ready for a new interview opportunity, ready for opportunity on the fly, and ready for things to change instantly for no particular reason. That is simply how it works.

If you understand that these challenges are a part of life and that they're not going away, things become much easier. If you're ready for as much as possible, at least what we can predict, it's going to make the process easier for you as you start a podcast. Get ready. Stay ready!

The Time is NOW!

I mentioned everything I did above about "shoulda, coulda, woulda" because the time is NOW. Yesterday is long gone;

right now is really all that we have, and tomorrow isn't guaranteed to anyone. *(READ THAT AGAIN.)*

Have you ever seen that image of a clock with no numbers on it? Instead of numbers it just says, the word "NOW"? Remind yourself next time you want to say I should be doing this, or 'I could be doing this.' or 'I would have done this.' Remember, The Time Is NOW."

Remember that next time you think of procrastinating.

What is possible if you start now? Right now? This time next year, you'll be able to look back and be glad that you decided to make a decision to take action now and not just talk about what you should be doing, could be doing, or would be doing. Remember, no one cares about what you should be doing, or what you would have done, or what you could do; they care about what you're doing NOW.

FYI... Tomorrow doesn't exist

Tomorrow is an absolute illusion. It's not guaranteed to any of us. We can look, we can plan, and we can hope but there is no guarantee that tomorrow will arrive. Thinking optimistically, of course, tomorrow is going to arrive, but if you continue to live your life in a space of tomorrow, you're telling yourself "I'll do it later." Did I mention the time is NOW?

"How soon not now becomes never."

-Martin Luther King, Sr.

The Present is a Gift

Yes, it sounds cheesy and cliche, but it is the truth. They call it the present because it simply is a gift, and it's all we have right now. Some would say life is empty and meaningless outside of the present moment, which is now, which is all we have. If you're thinking about yesterday, you're living in the past. If you're focused on today, you're living in the now, if you're focused on tomorrow, you're living in the future, the far distant future, even if it is tomorrow.

I found that being in the present moment really allows me to embrace the process of podcasting. It allows me to be as creative as possible. Yes, my mind wanders but it wanders on what is possible, pertaining to what I'm actually creating; the task at hand. Many times, we get stuck in what could have been rather than where we are in THIS moment, which is essentially all that we have. The present moment is extremely powerful, so make sure you take full advantage of it as you embark into your podcast launch journey.

You Either Want to do it or You Don't

It really is that simple: you either want it or you don't.

Just like you either want to read this book or you don't. Hopefully, you have gotten it into your head far enough, even this early on in the book, that you want to continue to better understand what's possible with starting a podcast.

I'm ridiculously humbled and grateful that you took time out of your day to pick up my book and read it. My hope and goal is to see you take this book and not just read, but actually do something with it.

Apparently, something inside you says, "I must start a podcast." If you follow what I teach you in this book, that's exactly what you're going to do. But it's going to take a lot of personal development in addition to acquiring knowledge about podcasting in order to start a podcast. You wouldn't believe the power behind procrastination. I will talk about it more extensively through the book.

WARNING: Procrastination will do one thing: keep you exactly where you are right now. Prolonged procrastination will continue to move you farther and farther away from where you actually want to be; starting a podcast. Don't give in to procrastination; it will win every time if you let it.

The time is now for you to start a podcast, and that's what this book is going to teach you. So let's get started!

Chapter 2
Getting Clear on Your WHY

It took me a long time to find my WHY.

Every time someone calls me and says, "I want to start a podcast," my first question is, "Why?" Most of the time, people are unclear as to their reason for starting a podcast. When this happens, I have to stop and encourage them to go back to the drawing board and get clear on why they want to start a podcast. Just because you think you have a good idea and it would be fun to start a podcast is not reason enough to start a podcast.

It took me nearly six years to figure out my big "Why?" Why am I doing the current work? Along with that came a lot of questions. What am I doing? Am I doing stuff that matters? Have I impacted peoples' lives? All the things that ran through my head. Oh, and I still couldn't figure it out. It took me six years to learn that the personal development I was doing was all part of the process which would eventually lead me to my "Why." I knew if I continued to show up, continued to do the work, and continued to focus on becoming the best version of myself, then everything would become clear, eventually.

No one can decide what your WHY is, if I told you what your why is, I would most likely be wrong, so I'm just going to encourage you to do what I did, ask yourself these simple questions...

- WHY DO I WANT TO START A PODCAST?
- WHO AM I SERVING WITH MY PODCAST?
- WHAT DO I WANT MY PODCAST TO DO FOR OTHERS?

There are some great resources available to help you map out your WHY. Two of my favorites are the books by Simon Sinek called *Start With Why* and *Find Your Why* (both available where books are sold).

It's going to take as long as it's going to take. Thinking or wishing you can rush the process usually only prolongs things. You've heard it before: "trust the process." It's so much easier to hear and say than actually do. What's possible if we trust the process? A lot; at least in my experience.

Starting a podcast is a very personal thing. I didn't realize that when I first started; I looked at it as just another piece of content for people to create as I embarked on the journey of launching the PodcastLaunchLab.com back in 2016. I quickly saw the evolution of people's interest changed on discovering their "Why I'm starting a podcast."

If I fast forward to the year 2020, I'm writing this book, approximately four years from when I started the PodcastLaunchLab. com. I took my time starting it because I wanted to figure out who my ideal client was. Once you're clear on who your ideal client is (or their avatar, if you will), then you know exactly who you're going after, and you also start to attract those types of people.

My why is extremely clear today. I have a podcast because I like to tell stories. And I like to tell other peoples' stories. Why do I have a podcast business? Because it enables me to empower, encourage, and provide a solution for people to tell their stories. Just like writing a book helps you leave a legacy for the world, I believe starting a podcast does the same thing. Podcast episodes don't exactly disappear (unless, of course, you delete them), but usually you're building a catalog of podcast episodes that will be there forever.

Just like a video or any other type of digital content, we are now documenting our lives for generations to come. We're documenting our life, we're documenting our experiences, we're documenting our work, we're documenting our branding, we're documenting each step along the journey through this thing called life.

It feels really good to figure out your why, for numerous reasons. The main one is that you're very, very clear on why you're doing what you're doing. Your intentions are clear, your vision is clear, and you are now ready to serve humanity by doing work that matters.

In this chapter, I'm going to dive deep into your why. You'll get really clear on the dynamics of why it's important to figure out your why, as redundant as that sounds.

Your WHY Empowers Other Peoples' WHY

One unique ability of being a leader (and a human being for that matter) is the opportunity to be able to encourage and empower people through the work you're doing. Figuring out your why could very well help someone understand what their why is and why they tuned into your podcast. They heard your story and something clicked for them; it was that moment where they connected with your content, with your why, and they were able to discover theirs. Now if that's not encouraging, I don't know what is. If that's not doing work that matters, then I'm clueless.

There's doing work you love, and then there's doing work you love that you know is impacting other people for the better. Who doesn't want to wake up every day knowing that the work they're doing is contributing to people actually making positive changes in life? A podcast is a gateway that is wide open for that type of opportunity, the type of opportunity to allow you to get very clear with your why. Launch a podcast to extract that why and expose it to a community in which other people can be impacted for the better.

This specific point in this chapter is one of my favorites. It's encouraging even to write these words, let alone have someone else read them! I know for a fact that my writing these words enables people to read these words and causes them to shift their mindset about getting clearer about their why. Not because they want to figure out their why. That's a given, but their why can actually enable other people to find out their why. You're reading this book to figure out how to start a podcast. Part of that process is figuring out your why. Little did you know that once your podcast is launched, and you're clear about your "why," you'll look back on this and laugh at any resistance given. It's funny how that works. To take things further, once you realize your podcast LED you to your why, and then your podcast, and then that process allowed you to do the same for others, it is most definitely a winning combination.

Finding Your WHY: How to do That

You may be thinking, "All of this sounds great, but what if I haven't found my why yet? How do I find my why? Is there a specific place I have to go for it?" Actually, there is. The place you're going to find your why is inside. Inside yourself, deep inside your heart, your soul, your mind. This isn't a book about personal development, but life is personal development. Taking on ventures like launching a podcast (when it's still kind of new and not really the norm yet) could feel a bit scary. That is unless of course, you're very clear about your why.

Let's talk about how you find your "Why." When you wake up in the morning and you think about that one thing you could do for the rest of your life; that pit in your stomach that's filled with excitement, hope, and optimism for the future; that's what your passion is, that's your why.

You could be a single parent and your why is wanting to give your child a better life than yours. If you had a rough past and you were able to recover, you want to share your story now with others. The clearer you can answer, the quicker you can answer that, the more your story will resonate with people who will be attracted to what you're doing. This, in its finest form is enrollment, enrollment into your why.

So, What is Your WHY?

The sooner you figure this out, the easier this process will be. For the rest of this chapter, I'm going to try my best to attempt to help you "Workshop Your Why."

I'd like you to take out a clean sheet of paper and a pen. At the top of the page, I want you to write: "My ideal life includes the following..."

If I had my dream job or dream business, I would be doing _____.

I feel the most fulfilled when I do _____.

My deepest desire is to _____.

Who do I Know Who has Figured Out Their Why and is Doing Work that Matters?

Once you list a few people you know who've done this, reach out to them, interview them. Even if it's a Zoom call, FaceTime, a text, or a phone call, just reach out to them. Let them know where you are in the process of starting a podcast. Tell them, "I'm reading a book that tells me finding my why is extremely important before starting a podcast. I've been encouraged to find other people who have already found their why, and get feedback from them.

What happens here? When you better understand other people's stories and other people's processes, this triggers things in our minds to help encourage the process of doing similar things yourself.

You'll find that when you're talking to individuals who have found their why, they're clearly doing work that they're passionate about and that matters to them. You'll find a common denominator. These individuals (as I do) want to encourage others to do the same thing. Chances are; they've done the work. They didn't just get lucky and find a reason why they did the work. They looked internally; inside themselves, and asked, "How can I do work that matters? Why am I doing the work that I am? Does it matter that I got very clear about these things and it's not something that just came naturally or just happened?" No, it doesn't. All that matters is finding your WHY.

Ask questions, be intuitive, be curious, and mildly relentless with figuring out your why.

This is all part of the process and the journey of figuring out who you are, before you start a podcast. Most of us have a community, the tribe and people around us. Some of us want to ask strangers for specific opinions. That's totally cool to do; you want to crowdsource other people who have figured out their why. Feel free to do so; post a question on Facebook, LinkedIn, or on Instagram asking people, "Are you doing work that matters? How do you know? Have you figured out your why?" People love to talk about themselves, so why not give them a platform to do so, and at the same time (based on the response they give you), you get one step closer to being clear on your why and one step closer to starting your podcast because you have the benefit of their experience.

It doesn't have to be just one person. It can be several. Interview people constantly. People you know, people you don't know; friends of friends, whatever the case is. Just evaluate how other people did what you're trying to do. Not in the same way because you are you and they are them, but we're all here to be in community, to serve each other and support each others' lives.

These answers may not come to you immediately; that's why I've encouraged you to take out a piece of paper. Don't just take out your phone and pull out a note and type it. I want you to actually write these things down on a piece of paper. Studies have shown writing things down allows our brain to consume significantly more than we would by being stuck to our device (which most of us are 24 hours a day 7 days a week, outside of sleeping. Of course, some people even wake up to check their phone, I'm guilty of that, but that's a whole other chapter, maybe even a whole other book!).

Be with these questions. Don't try to answer them right now, unless, of course, the answers are showing up for you.

Remember that everything you need; you already possess.

You can't force figuring these things out. I say that because I speak from experience. I used to get so frustrated with myself, I used to get so frustrated at life, I used to get so upset that I wasn't where I thought I should be. I'm eternally grateful for all of that frustration in the past.

All of those things I was completely unclear about taught me patience, resilience, and to trust the process every time. I want to say ***You're the only one who can discover it***.

We may be able to give some perspective, but you're the only one who can get clear on what your why is for starting a podcast. You're the only one who can get clear on what your why is for doing work that matters. You're the only one who can get clear on how you're going to serve people by getting clear on your why and living out your purpose and passion as a human being.

We are just passing through this life; it doesn't last forever. Our time is limited; all of our time is limited. So wouldn't you want to spend every moment striving to be the best version of yourself?

A thought which runs through my head constantly, in addition to making sure I'm still clear with my why, is that I'm still doing work that matters. I am always curious about the impact I'm having on the people I'm working with.

The power of your why changes people's lives. But you have to believe that. If you don't believe it, no one else will. Believing in yourself, believing in the work you're doing, and believing in your why have the utmost importance and should be a priority in your life. Without them, you're not going to be able to engage anyone in what you think should be done.

Do you understand WHY I wrote this chapter now? (Insert LOL here.)

It was a small pun involved with the point I just mentioned. LOL (I'm not sure you can include LOL in books, but I just did). All kidding aside, I really hope you understand now why I wrote this chapter in this book. It's why I extensively speak to the topic of figuring out your why as part of your podcast journey.

I'd like to invite you to consider this: your podcast is going to be one of the most motivating things you've ever done for yourself and for others. I want you to think as you continue to read through this book what the possibilities are pertaining to you getting clear on your why and figuring out your passion, and then pursuing your passion by launching a podcast. I commend you for taking a step in this direction.

Not everyone is brave enough to dig deep and figure out their WHY. I want to serve humanity and do work that matters. You may be reading this book, and you already have started your podcast. You may not even know what a podcast is, but reading this book will have helped you better understand what you don't know. That you don't know about your why, about your passion, about serving people, about podcasting, and about doing work that matters.

Part of writing a book is writer's block. I've experienced plenty of it, and I'm only on chapter 2! Instead of getting frustrated with not being able to figure out what I want to talk about, I walk away from my writing, regroup, and come back to it.

Writer's block was not part of this chapter. I sat down, and I knew the process was about finding your why and how important it is in the podcasting journey. Having already experienced this process and going through it myself (and continuing to go through it), I can tell you that writer's block comes because your why today isn't always your why tomorrow or next year. Your reason for helping people may not be the same today as it will be next month, next year, three years from now, five years from now, so it's always good to stop and check in and ask yourself, "Why am I doing the work that

I'm doing? Why did I start a podcast? What is it doing for people? Am I doing work that matters?"

Checking in constantly on yourself to refresh your mind. People change and evolve. It is important to stay true to ourselves and to those people whom we are serving.

So, get excited about your why! Even if you haven't figured out what it is just yet. You will, I promise. And when you do, you're going to be even more excited than you are right now by simply reading this chapter. You may be reading this book and thinking, "I didn't even know I had to get clear on a why or my passion before I started a podcast." Part of that is true, some people will start a podcast without getting clear on their why, without getting clear on their passion, without getting clear on why they're doing the actual act of starting a podcast. I'm trying to prevent all of that. I want people to do work that matters. I want individuals just like you to get clear on their why because I've been able to encourage and empower; to give some feedback as to the power behind finding your why.

When you have found your own why, it's exciting when someone else finds their why because of something you did to help impact their life... it's even more exciting! Anchor that feeling in, do it right now; what it feels like, what it will feel like to get clear on your why. After that, what does it look like to impact other people's lives because you got clear on your why and you executed on it? That, my friends, is called doing work that matters. There's nothing more powerful than figuring something out for ourselves. Then; being able to share it with others and have them enroll in the same process and make similar adjustments and see similar results as to what you did.

I think I've talked enough about your why and your passion. All of that matters when starting a podcast. Now it's time to get out there and go figure out your why. I gave you some practical steps above, especially the ones you're going to include on a fresh journal entry or a blank sheet of paper. Ask yourself some intuitive questions that really get you thinking and feeling in specific ways and write down both the questions and your answers.

Doing so, you will start to jog your mind and emotions in an effort to bring you closer to figuring out what your why is. Seeing you start a podcast is extremely encouraging. Seeing you find your why blows that process out of the water. Seeing you do both makes all the work I do worth it. I don't know if anybody has told you this or not, but yes you can! Yes, YOU CAN find your why! Yes, YOU CAN start a podcast! Yes, YOU CAN be passionate and do work that helps other people do the same thing! It all starts with X finding Y. See what I did there? (Wink.)

Chapter 3
Being ALL-IN with Podcasting

Let me be the first one to say: when I started my podcast, I thought I was going to go all-in, but I was far from it. In fact, I started and stopped my podcast three times before I finally decided I was going to commit to it and that I was simply going to go all-in with podcasting. The majority of my decision was based on the fact that I was going to go all-in with podcasting for my business, not just to have a podcast. Not remaining consistent, not going all-in with my podcast while trying to sell someone a solution to start a podcast simply didn't toe the line. I knew that I had to stick with it this time. After all; third time's a charm, right?

What have I learned? Just this: It really doesn't matter how long it takes you to get there, just as long as you get there. Had I not started and stopped my show three times, I would never have ended up where I am now with the mindset and perspective on going all-in. I not only have my own podcast, but also a podcast business, The PodcastLaunchLab.com, which helps marketers and entrepreneurs go from idea to iTunes in 90 days or less.

I'm a storyteller as part of my personal brand. As a speaker, author, trainer, and coach, my passion is telling stories. Therefore, my podcast is called the "Beyond the Story" podcast, where I go beyond telling people's ordinary story of how they got to where they are right now, to a better understanding of how the story came together.

Why Part-time Works, But Doesn't

When I was younger, I was in my sales manager's office. I asked if I could work part-time, and he replied, "How about 'no time?" We both laughed, but that's really funny when you think about sales. Talk about a job that can't be done part-time; it's most definitely sales. Now don't get me wrong; can you sell something with a part-time job? Absolutely. Maybe as a retail associate or selling cable television door-to-door. Maybe you get lucky for putting in the effort, but I don't believe you're going to be able to earn any type of significant income working part-time in the world of sales. Unless, of course, you're selling something that's yours.

I use this example of sales because most people can relate to it. I experienced having a podcast over the past 10 years part-time, automatically making my podcast sit on the back burner. It's just something I did. Don't get me wrong; if podcasting is a hobby, if this is something you want to do on nights or weekends because you enjoy it, then by all means, go nuts. This book is for individuals looking to start a podcast, to grow a podcast, monetize a podcast, and be an extension (if not a business) as part of their brand.

More times than not, when we put half the effort in, we get half of the results. Part-time works great if it's for a second job that you need in order to make ends meet. However, when it comes to podcasting, or any content creation project for that matter, it requires your full commitment.

When you're inconsistent with your podcast, think about your audience. If someone loves your content, who are you to prevent them from consuming more content? Simply because you didn't get around to it or didn't fulfill your own commitment of staying consistent with your podcast?

Keep your audience in mind. Your community in mind. These are the individuals who are going to help your show grow and continue.

Why You Want to Be ALL-IN with Podcasting

That commitment time is created for you, but whatever it is, stick to it and go all in.

There are no formal rules when deciding how much time is going to be required when you start your podcast, just create a realistic time frame: a realistic amount of time you can commit to your podcast on an ongoing basis and stick to it. Full time just simply means you're going to stick to the amount of time you've created and allowed to get your podcast started.

I think the odds are forever in our favor when we make a decision to go all-in with our efforts on what we're doing, especially something like starting a podcast. Creating content and starting a podcast is no easy task, but it's not impossible. However, it does require a tremendous amount of commitment on our end.

- Commit: we're actually going to start the podcast.
- Commit: we're actually going to record episodes.
- Commit: we're actually going to keep the show going.

You must set yourself up for success when starting a podcast, and the best way to do that, like I've been alluding to, is leveraging yourself. Making sure that those closest to you are holding you accountable, are clear about your intentions and goals as far as starting a podcast; this will help tremendously. You'll start to hear things like, "Hey, when's the new episode coming out? How's the new podcast coming along? When does your new podcast start?" When you start talking about your podcast before it's there, you start to enroll people in it.

How to be ALL-IN with Podcasting

Wouldn't it be great if we could just wave some magic wand and automatically be all in on something of our choice, like starting a podcast? One can dream. On the flip side of things,

I say we create our own magic wand. We wave it ourselves, enable and empower ourselves because we believe in what we're doing, and we believe in what the vision of the podcast is all about. Therefore, we have no other option for ourselves than to be all in with our podcast.

The lesson here, make your own magic wand and wave it yourself. Be ALL in. You can't have just one foot in the door.

Think for a second back to a time when you went all in on something. How did it make you feel? How did you feel about yourself and the overall outlook on what you decided to pursue when you went all-in? What did your peers, friends, and family say? What did those closest to you say to you? How did they show up? How did that feel when they did?

Just like starting a podcast for the sake of having a podcast, there is no cookie-cutter way of determining how to be all in with podcasting. In my experience, making up my mind and strategically setting myself up for success, aligning myself with people who I want interview, getting on their calendar, occupying time on someone else's calendar and also booking it on mine allowed me not only to remain consistent but also allowed me to continue to go all-in with my podcast.

Do you want to be all in with your podcast? Then set realistic goals for yourself and your show. Align yourself with people you want to interview on your show. Schedule and commit to the interview and get the episode recorded.

Reap the Rewards of "ALL-IN"

I'm not saying going all-in guarantees success on any type of venture, but there are several success stories that have taken place due to someone making a commitment to go all-in with what they were doing, all in with starting a podcast, all in with launching their personal brand, all in on starting the company they've always dreamed of doing.

The common denominator here is; ALL-IN.

I could go on and on about what the rewards are of being able to achieve our goals and being able to go all-in. For the purposes of podcasting, I want to chat about what the rewards of going all-in with your podcast can be.

First, if you go all in and stay consistent, you're going to have a podcast. I mean, that is the goal, correct? Next on the list, you're going to make brand-new connections with people you're interviewing on your show, people you are getting to know by default because you're interviewing them. You're picking their brain in a very constructive way while stroking their ego and making it all about them (or at least it should be).

Next, you're building a community and a listenership, which, in the future, can be monetized with sponsors, advertisers, and strategic revenue-generating tactics to make your show or turn your show into an actual business. Being all in produces a podcast with new connections and a community podcast that you can monetize. Are there any questions?

How can you start today being "ALL IN" about your podcast?

- Commit to a start date
- Create a schedule of upcoming episodes
- Reach out to future guests and get them scheduled for the show; COMMIT!
- Enroll people in your community, into your effort and vision for the show!

Start with those four basic steps. You'll see the steps require you actually taking a piece of paper and pen and writing things down. There's something to be said when we're been able to sit down with a pen and a piece of paper, and plan out exactly what we have envisioned for the podcast. If you start with a commitment to have a start date, write that day down. Put it on a Post-It in your bathroom. Put it on Post-Its around your house, in front of your monitor. Seeing it constantly keeps it fresh in your mind and enrolls yourself first. Then you can enroll others by default.

Next, make a plan for your episodes; literally write out a plan for each episode. Episode 1, Title, Guest Questions, Notes. Feel free to add any additional information you need to when you're scripting out each episode. The more information the better but keep it to one page; you don't want five pieces of paper in front of you when you're trying to record and remember everything you want to talk about. Make it easy on yourself, make sure it flows, create a system that works for you, and don't forget to create and plan out each and every episode.

This is absolutely vital to the ongoing success of your broadcast. Once this is done, you're ready to start reaching out to people and asking them if they're open to being a guest on your podcast. Make it all about them. Talk about what they do, what their goals are, what their business is, what their focus is. Once you make it all about them, they're far more open to being a guest and doing whatever it takes to help you market the episode they're on.

Reaching out to people and scheduling appointments for your podcast does a couple of things beyond the obvious development of content. It allows you to connect with people that you don't know. These people should be people who are smarter than you are and have accomplished more than you. They can really speak some insight into the interview when you have them on the show and you're talking about their story.

Another reason for reaching out to people and booking them for the show: You create a finite date where both parties commit to being on the podcast, so you're now on the hook, as is your guest you've booked. Get the mindset that "I'm on someone else's schedule and canceling or rescheduling is simply rude." Another phenomenal example of being able to set yourself up for success: create leverage on yourself and enroll others in the process. When you schedule people and have them on your podcast, you are enrolling them into your process by default.

Let's talk about what happens during the interview. Conversations have a tendency to go in several different directions, and, as the host, you want to keep things as organized as possible. But when you have someone on your show and you're interviewing them, this is a form of picking someone's brain constructively in a very productive way. How cool is it to know you reached out to someone you admire and you now have them on your show? You can ask them whatever you'd like! Some may consider this picking someone's brain; some simply interviewing the guest. The choice is yours.

Later in the book, I will go in greater deal on the best practice for conducting an interview with someone. Until then, keep reading!

Chapter 4
PROCRASTINATION, Why Waiting to Start a Podcast Is a TERRIBLE Idea

The very fact that podcasts have been around for over 15 years and are just now gaining popularity is reason in and of itself for you not to procrastinate and sleep on starting a podcast. At the time I'm writing this book, there are just over 1 million podcasts. That number was just achieved, as the number of podcasts hovered around 800,000 for quite some time up until late 2019.

If we compare this to the number of creators on YouTube, that number is extremely low. YouTube has approximately 15 million YouTube creators on the platform. Those are people with channels creating content. Compare 15 million creators to 1 million podcasters. I say there's quite the market available for you to start a podcast. The time is now, not tomorrow, not next week, and next month, not next year. Because soon enough, you're going to realize everyone, and their brother is starting a podcast. There is something to be said with being the first within your vertical, or one of the first within your vertical or business or brand to start a podcast before your competition has done so. Starting now is going to put you far ahead of the game when podcasting actually does become mainstream and everyone and their brother is starting one.

Remember your WHY? Great.

Another great way to fend off procrastination is to remember your why. We talked a lot about your WHY earlier in this book, and I'm going to continue to talk about your why throughout the book. Your WHY, like I mentioned before, is extremely powerful. So powerful, it can actually put the ball into action and be a constant reminder of why you must start a podcast. Especially if you have a story to tell and impactful content to share; people are waiting to hear that. I always say, "You're a taker if you have a story to tell that can impact people's lives and you refuse to tell it ." You're doing no one any favors and actually doing yourself a disservice. The world wants to hear your story. The world needs your story. So, why wait?

Every time you want to put the good ol' podcast on the back burner, remind yourself of your why. You're probably reading this and thinking, "I don't even have my why yet, so I guess I would be qualified to procrastinate."

No, you just haven't discovered your why yet. That's something you need to focus on if you are going to get serious and start a podcast. Anchor every single one of your motives for starting a podcast and continuing your podcast with your why. I say that because it's extremely powerful and keeps us centered and focused on why we started with a project in the first place. You are starting a podcast because you're clear you want to serve people. That feeling anchors deep inside us and motivates us to want to continue, because this podcast, this platform, or this content is not about us. It's about the people consuming the content in the podcast and the lives being changed because of it.

Many times throughout the process of writing this book, I have wanted to procrastinate.

Many times while writing this book, I did procrastinate. I set a goal to write this book in 90 days. If I continued to procrastinate and push things off, not do the work, and not stay committed to my mission that I'm writing a book to help people better understand what they don't know about starting a podcast, I would never get this book done. No one is immune from procrastination, it's human nature. Just focus on not making it a habit.

Procrastination also is a choice. All of us do it. We decide to do it. We decide to not do it. There is no maybe, there is no try, there is no ancillary word to insert here to justify procrastination. Procrastination is great when you're responding to someone because you're upset. Procrastination is great when you're in college and you have a boyfriend or a girlfriend and you're are madly in love, but you decide to get through college and find a job first before you're actually going to settle down and seriously buy a house, have kids, etc. Those are about the only times procrastination really comes into play and we can utilize it to our advantage. Otherwise, it's simply holding us back. I don't know about you, but I don't like to be held back with anything, including starting a podcast.

One thing I really like to do when I'm considering procrastination, is put myself in the shoes of my future self actually accomplishing the task I've been procrastinating about. I think and meditate on what it will feel like to know I didn't want to do it, but I ended up doing it, and now I'm glad I did. That is a rewarding feeling, which is something we have to create on our own; it's not something which comes naturally to us.

"Yesterday, you said tomorrow."

-Nike

One of my favorite campaigns from Nike is a billboard they posted some years ago which simply said, "Yesterday, you said tomorrow." How many times do we find ourselves saying, "I'll do it tomorrow, I'll do it next week, I'll do it next month, I'll do it next year." It's a pretty consistent response to life for most of us (again, human nature), but it's still a choice.

When was the last time you said, "I'll do it tomorrow." Yesterday? It probably happened today or probably sometime this week. If it hasn't, it will. Unless, of course, you can make a decision to shift your mindset and make a commitment to following through with your original plan, which is starting a podcast.

FYI... the Time is NOW!

Time, it's the only thing they're not making more of. The time is now! You're going to hear me mention that several times throughout this book, and for good reason. There is no time for procrastination when you're trying to figure out how to start a podcast (or how to launch anything, for that matter). We've covered procrastination in this chapter, but now I really want to anchor down the idea that the time is NOW. Yesterday's gone, tomorrow isn't here yet. That means RIGHT NOW is all we have.

Maybe You've Been Looking For a Sign -This is it

There's also power in now. There's power in believing something can be done right in this second; not tomorrow, not next week, not next month, not next year. Think about this for a second: if you actually started something right now and put full effort and commitment into it, what would be possible? I think a lot of times, we never stop and think how powerful the moment of now really is. There are numerous times in the past we've taken action immediately, because we are emotionally driven and motivated, automatically committed to whatever it is we wanted to do.

The same amount of effort which goes into all those spontaneous opportunities can go into something that's intentional and thought out. You've been thinking about this idea for years, let today be the day you're finally going to get started. Why? Because you're embracing the now.

There aren't very many times in life we say, "You know, I'm really glad I didn't take advantage of something in the present moment and missed on an opportunity." I don't want to say that's a mistake. I don't believe there are any mistakes, they're simply lessons for us to learn. But there are missed opportunities, for sure. Opportunities we ignore, opportunities that pass by, opportunities that we see, we know we should do, and we completely ignore the opportunity in our hands. Then, we look back and wonder, "What happened?" If you're in a space where you take full ownership of your life, you'll realize you didn't take advantage of that opportunity, and there's no one to blame but yourself. We've all been there; chances are, we'll be there again.

The very fact you're reading this book is reason enough for you to do something for yourself, for your future, for your family's future, now. I've emphasized the power of now for a specific reason. People write books on this topic, people quote this topic, and for good reason. Everything else is just a made-up illusion outside of right now; yesterday's gone; full of memories, challenges, lessons, and missed opportunities. Today is right here, right now for us to own leverage and take full advantage of. Tomorrow doesn't even exist until, of course, we get there, and then it'll just be another opportunity to be in the now and in the present.

I'm here to say this book is not a personal development book, but I believe you have to personally develop in order to become who you need to be for whatever brand or whatever mission you're launching or setting up to get your message out. You have to be whole as a human, and you have to be willing to do the work and take full ownership of your life. That way, you know how to respond and how to work in community with others. Others may not see eye-to-eye with your thought process; that's the beauty of community! Being able to exchange ideas and constantly having our thoughts and ideas challenged and contributed to.

What in the World are You Waiting For?!

Have you ever stopped to ask yourself what you're waiting for? It's a pretty fascinating question to ask yourself. If you can answer that, then you can, more than likely, take action on what you have or have not done. Forget about the lack thereof, or how long it takes you to finally get started. The important part is starting. The last thing you want to do is wait, and rinse and repeat what you've always done. Waiting, just letting time fly by knowing you have everything in your power to do something and stop waiting, but you don't, in my opinion, that's a very scary place to be. If you're there and you're reading this right now, I encourage you to dig deep and ask yourself a very very honest question: "What am I waiting for?"

There is no perfect time, there is no perfect set date. Waiting just pushes off, even disintegrates the goals and dreams we have. The longer we wait, the less motivated we are to pursue them, and suddenly, time's up.

But what about the people who want to hear your message? What about the people who want to hear your podcast? Their minds shift. They want to be encouraged -- all because you did not procrastinate, they can now listen to your podcast. These are all things that happen when you make the decision to not procrastinate on the things you know you should do!

All of this is possible. This is not a fairytale. This is all reality. IF you're willing to step into the reality that is starting a podcast and telling your story, then building a community, and connecting with people, will help them take your story and improve their life.

When you embrace the fact it takes work to start a podcast, but you're more concerned about helping other people, the workload is not going to seem so heavy. In fact, it'll lighten things, just by the simple fact you're focused on service, serving people, and doing good. Starting a podcast is one of the best things you can do as a human and for humanity, especially if you've got a story to tell. Your goal is to reach people and tell them your story and watch their life change for whatever reason that may be.

Your Competition Will Not Wait

Podcasting has been around for over 15 years now and was very popular when it first started. Then, years later, it has became even more popular (I'd say around 2008), and here we are. As I'm writing this book, it's 2020, and there are approximately 1 million podcasts. Podcasting is replacing radio. Podcasting will, in fact, be the new frontier on how brands, individuals, people, companies, and communities get the word out about what they do and what their stories are all about, while building a community.

If you think your competition is going to sleep on the opportunity of starting a podcast once it starts to become mainstream, you've got another think coming. Just like everything else that becomes popular, there was a point in time when businesses didn't even want to use fax machines. Then fax machines were all the rage. Now they've been phased out, for the most part, and new technology provides the opportunity to be able to get a document instantly. Now smartphones have replaced almost any old technology tool.

Technology doesn't slow down for any of us, but we, in turn, evolve with that technology. At least most of us do.

The same applies for marketing. Social media platforms, media of any type, are the new opportunity to get the word out, and brands are going to take full advantage of it. Why? Because the magazine ad, the newspaper ad, the radio ad, and the TV ad aren't giving anywhere close to the results they used to, are they?

Still, one would argue yes, and another would argue no. As it happens, your competition will naturally join the herd to tell their story and create content and leverage their brand to become a media company by having a podcast. If you take out a sheet of paper and write down your competition right now and do quick research to see whether or not they have a podcast, you'll be pleased to see that most of them do not. What does this mean for you? It means the first mover's advantage. That's been a good advantage since business was business.

Should, Coulda, Woulda - Where Else Does This Show Up in Your Life?

Shoulda. Coulda. Woulda. How many times have you said those words or heard those words? Happens all the time. "I should be doing this, I could be doing this, I would be doing this..." All simply lines of hot air. Why? Because they do nothing. They provoke no action. They don't talk about what is actually happening and what they're actually doing.

That's what these words do for us. I strongly encourage you to keep these words completely out of your vocabulary and focus just on the things that you know are possible for you to start. The things you know you can absolutely execute on and make happen with certainty. Your awareness of these three words constantly leads to you running every idea through this filter in your mind. Every time you think about an idea or something that you want to start (specifically a podcast), ask yourself how long you have been talking about a podcast, saying, "I should start a podcast. I could start a podcast. I would start a podcast but. . . but. . . but. . . but. . ."

Self-awareness really comes into play when we talk about launching things like a podcast or a YouTube channel, or creating a type of content where we're going to use our voice and leverage it to create content, build a community around that content, and impact the community with our content. I've always found that taking the words "Shoulda Coulda Woulda" out of my vocabulary allows me to stay present with myself and honest, as far as my intentions on the projects I take on. We all take on things we start and never finish. The things that really matter sometimes fall into that category too; that's why it's important to be aware of the things you're saying "Yes" to, the commitments you're making. Are you in this podcasting thing for the long haul? Or is this something you want to continue to do, year after year after year, and watch it grow?

See what happens and see where it goes or you're not really sure is NOT a suggested approach.

If you actually said, "I'm not really sure," I'm going to suggest that you go back and read the first few chapters.

I hope this chapter encouraged you to not wait to pursue your podcasting dreams. The time truly is NOW. You could literally put this book down and start writing your show and creating RIGHT NOW. There's no excuse; not an equipment excuse, not a hosting excuse, and not an internet excuse (unless of course, you don't have internet. Then you'll need to figure that out, because in order to have a podcast, internet is most definitely useful).

I wrote this chapter so we can keep it real with each other and keep it honest and keep it transparent. I share all this based on one thing: personal experience. I would never have the audacity to write a book telling you what to do if I had not experienced it in the first place.

I hope you're encouraged that we're only 4 chapters in with 7 to go! The good news is, it's only going to get better. You're only going to be more encouraged and more excited to actually make your podcasting dreams come true.

Remember, that sign you were looking for was this chapter.

Chapter 5
What it Takes to Start A Podcast

By now you know you should be clear on your why. Having your why dialed in, knowing exactly the reason for starting your podcast, is extremely powerful. You've done that work.

Now it's time to get serious and start unpacking the process of actually starting a podcast. That's right, I'm going to walk you through step-by-step every step of the way in order to help you and to teach you how to launch your own podcast. The steps that I'm going to teach you are the same steps we take to launch a podcast at the PodcastLaunchLab.com. Where we take them from idea to iTunes in 90 days or less with this process.

The reason our business exists is because people don't have the time to learn on their own or would rather pay someone to professionally coach them, instruct them, and help them produce the podcast that they're launching. The reason I bring this up is not to brag about the PodcastLaunchLab.com being a "one stop shop" (although we are really awesome; we know that).

Our goal is to help you better understand that it requires no outside effort for you to launch a podcast. I mean zero outside effort.

"It's always a good time to start a podcast"

-Seth Godin

Seth Godin's one of my favorite marketers and authors. This quote is one of my favorites, so I found it appropriate to share before we begin the process of helping you better understand how to start a podcast from A to Z.

Step 1: Create a Show Name

First things first in the podcast launch process is creating a name. You're starting a podcast, so your podcast is going to need a name. But it's not just any name; this isn't an AOL screen name from the mid-2000s. This is an extension of your brand, whether it be your personal brand, your business brand, or maybe even a mix of both. You want to come up with something that compliments that: something catchy, something memorable, something that will resonate with people.

I'm a digital storyteller, I interview people and tell their stories in addition to mine. My podcast has recently been rebranded to the BeyondTheStoryPodcast.com, so it aligns with my brand because I'm a storyteller. I give you that example so you can better understand what a good fit might be for yourself. I strongly advise that you come up with a couple of different ideas and take a poll both online or maybe to your email list of friends, family, and people who tell you the truth. Get honest feedback on the ideas that you think are absolutely amazing but that others may give you some not so comfy feedback. In the end, it ends up paying off to your benefit.

I want to be clear that the name of your podcast is going to be an extension of your brand. But that doesn't necessarily mean that it's going to be the same name as your brand. The choice is entirely up to you. I highly suggest that you send your ideas to a few people to get their opinion. Feedback is extremely valuable. People love to give their opinion, whether it's ego-based or fact-based, but getting feedback when you're fleshing something out like graphic design or a branding name is critical. It is very important to get feedback because you can find yourself preventing a significant number of challenges moving forward.

For example, launching your podcast thinking it's the greatest name in the world and then later realizing that it just doesn't resonate with people because when you say the name of your podcast people look at you like you have 10 heads.

I share this example from past experience. My podcast was originally called "SocialBuzzONAIR." I started and stopped my show three times over the past 10 years, and through that process, switched things up with the name. I just felt that I could. That was not the best way to approach things, as the third time that I launched my podcast, I called it "The Seb Rusk Show."

First of all, people don't even know how to pronounce Seb, which is simply short for Sebastian. I found myself at a podcast conference earlier in 2020, and people would constantly ask me the name of my show. I would say, "I'm a digital storyteller. It's called The Seb Rusk Show," and people would slowly nod their head forward, and say, "Oh, cool. Sounds great." This would leave me feeling, "Wow, they don't even know what my show is about. I don't even know what my show is, but I guess my name isn't working."

The very next week, I said "this ends here." We're changing the name of the show." I'm a storyteller. So I sat, and I brainstormed. I mind mapped ideas, and I searched iTunes to see what there was already to make sure I wouldn't be overlapping something. Eventually, I came up with "Beyond The Story." Everyone has a story, but I like to have conversations with people on my show to talk about different aspects of their story, different aspects of their journey in life, different aspects of what they've done or how they've accomplished something.

Lastly, I strongly suggest that you have ideas, three to five different ideas, and spend time with them. Think about them, evaluate them, and then reach out for feedback. This way, you can get real clear on what the name should be. We name our kids, pets, cars, and we know when we've come up with the right name.

Remember, just because you think it's an awesome name, that doesn't mean it's an awesome name. Your podcast name really has nothing to do with you and everything to do with your audience. You want to make sure you're focused on engaging with the person who will be consuming your content. How do they think of or perceive your brand and name; as in what do they think when they hear your podcast name?

These are all things to consider when coming up with your awesome podcast show name.

Step 2: Design Your Cover Art

Now that you have a name down, it's time to create the branding for your show. Some call it album cover art or podcast art, or a podcast logo. Now, the WHY of you're starting your podcast will determine exactly how your album art is designed.

If you choose to use a free platform like Anchor.FM, then you have the opportunity to design your own album art from within the Anchor.FM platform.

I recommend you hire a freelancer and go to a freelance site like Fiverr or Upwork or Freelancer.com and find a designer to suit your needs. You'll pay them anywhere between $15 and $50 to create your album art. This investment is important but not required, and you can get it done very economically if you find the right designer, especially on fiverr.com. I love to use Fiverr, but there are also other popular freelancer platforms like UpWork.com that will produce the same result.

Search for podcast cover art, podcast logo, album cover art, find a designer that can fulfill what you need, which is designing your album cover, aka your podcast logo. I'm using Fiverr as an example because it's one of the most popular freelance platforms available today. I used to freelancers a lot, too, but I seem to have better talent and be better able to communicate my message when I have a designer that shares my vision when I use someone on Fiverr.com.

Before you go hiring any freelancers, I would definitely log on to Canva.com, one of my favorite platforms. It allows just about anyone to become a graphic designer based on the tools and resources available that it can provide. You can literally become a graphic designer in minutes. I think Canva. com costs about $12 a month, and there may be a free version as well. It's extremely limited, but it still allows you to get in and create something. It is your best shot when you never know what you'll end with. I ended up designing the first version of my new album art for Beyond the Story podcast in Canva.com

After that, I sent it over to a freelance graphic designer, to polish it up, give it a fresh look and add to it. There are no rules for your podcast cover art other than the fact that you don't want to put a podcast microphone or headphones on the art just because it's a podcast, unless of course it's a podcast about podcasting.

Your cover art will have the name of your show, possibly a picture of you or your co-host or your logo for your business or brand. I do want to emphasize that your cover art must look clean, professional, and appealing. Just like it's critical that your podcast name must resonate with people, your podcast art is even more important.

Why? Because your podcast cover art is the very first thing someone sees when they go through podcasts. Whether it's on Spotify, iHeartRadio, iTunes, or another platform, your podcast cover and your podcast description on the episode are the only ways to create a strong first impression for people to say, "I want to listen to this podcast!"

Like several other steps in the process, I recommend that you poll people whose opinions you trust. Talk to friends, family members, the ones who tell you the truth and will give you honest feedback on the design of your album art. It may even be a good idea to just put a small group of options together for three to five people and walk them through the whole process. Give them something in exchange for their feedback.

I must caution you that you need to be prepared for that feedback to not be 100% positive. Because we think our ideas are the greatest ideas in the world, but they aren't always, are they? Often when we ask people we trust for their opinion and they give their honest opinion, we are offended. Don't get offended. Stay open to honest negative feedback.

Things can always be improved, and you can't see your own blind spots. This is a major key in the creative process, being able to identify blind spots and correct them. In this case, it's launching an awesome podcast. The people you engage for their opinion are a vital part of your podcast launch process. It's important to understand people want to help, they want to give feedback, they want to give their opinion. We get this from their ego or simply from a very transparent space, or sometimes both.

Step 3: Write Your INTRO and OUTRO Scripts

The next step in the podcast launch process is creating the intro and outro scripts for your podcast. These are the sound bites that go before the episode starts and at the end. While they're not required, it is standard protocol to have a standard introduction to your show. The introduction gets people fired up and excited and gives them a bit of information of what to expect from the show based on the type of show that it is.

It goes a little something like this. "Welcome to my podcast show. My podcast is about baskets, so if you love baskets, then you're in the right place. And now here's your host, Sebastian."

An outro sounds like this: "Thanks so much for tuning in to my podcast. I sure do appreciate it, if you haven't done so already, make sure you subscribe to the show wherever you listen to podcasts. This way you'll get notified as new episodes become available. Thanks again for tuning in, and we'll talk to you next time."

As you can see, this is a very precise way of greeting your podcast listeners and also sending your listeners off when they're done listening to the episode. Some people like to get creative with their outro and say some sort of offer or call to action, for example, "Thanks so much tuning into this episode of my podcast. I sure do appreciate it."

This way, you can give some sort of call to action and send people somewhere specific for your outro. This is not required, but it is good information to know in the event you have some sort of offer or some sort of call to action to provide in your outro, which you should.

I'm not sure that an outro is the place to try to sell something unless your show has grown to the point that you're able to monetize it with sponsors and advertisers. If that's the case, maybe an advertisement of some sort during your outro would be okay. If you follow this simple format of greeting your listeners by writing an intro and sending your listeners off by thanking them for the show through your outro, then you'll have exactly what you need for a podcast intro and outro.

Step 4: Podcast Equipment

People constantly get hung up on the idea of having some sort of complicated equipment. Seriously; you can record a podcast on an iPhone 6 and produce it. I bring this up because I don't want you to over complicate the process of equipment for your podcast.

The earbuds that come with a cord with every iPhone on the planet will work. So will any quiet place that doesn't have a lot of echo or background noise. I used to record a lot in my closet because it's a very muffled area, almost like being in the sound booth. But any room with carpet that doesn't have high ceilings or concrete floors should be sufficient for you to be able to record your podcast.

I've found that most people would rather have at least some sort of USB microphone. In that case, you can check out a Blue Snowball microphone which will run you between $60 and $75 and up from there. Another good product is the Blue Yeti, which will run you around $120 or $130. These microphones are USB microphones. They are condenser mics that condense the sound and make you sound more professional. Both of them are available on Amazon.com or sweetwater.com.

Something more advanced I would recommend is the Focusrite Scarlett 2i2 studio. It'll run you about $285, but it comes with a condenser mic with XLR microphone cable that plugs into a box. That small box, about the size of two decks of cards plugs into your computer via USB. This is literally an instant studio set up with any microphone. This is an actual professional XLR condenser and/or dynamic microphone but you get the best of both worlds because the box plugs directly into your computer. This product is available on Amazon. com.

Remember, don't overthink the podcast microphone. It's not that complicated, and if you have a new phone and a quiet space, you're off to the races!

Step 5: Record Your Intro and Outro

After you write your intro and outro script, it's time to record your intro and outro. This can be done by a third party, or it can be done by you. It's entirely up to you.

Once again, Fiverr.com is another great way to find an audio editor who can help create an intro and outro for your podcast. A lot of them will provide the voiceover and music for it. The music should get people excited to listen to the episode and also glad they listened to the episode. You can choose any way that you'd like, whether you do it yourself or use a male or female to create a specific style or energy level. All these choices are entirely up to you.

If you want to keep things simple with your intro and outro, you can simply record your intro yourself into your iPhone's voice recorder. Send that voiceover to an editor on Fiverr and ask him to add music to the back. In no time, you'll have an intro and outro for between $25 to $100, depending on which editor you choose to use of those available. One of the best tactics to follow when trying to find a new audio editor is to review their profile and look at past projects that they've done. If I like the sound of the intros and outros they provided to those clients, I know chances are I'm going to end up with a great product for my intro and outro, too.

Step 6: Find Background Music

Like I mentioned above, I highly recommend hiring an audio editor to do the editing and creation of your intro and outro. Write the script, record it, send it to an editor who can edit it and find royalty-free music for you.

If you want to do this yourself, you totally can, especially if you're using a platform like AnchorFM. Anchor allows you to record with ease.

You can record your intro, you can record your outro, and you can save the files on the computer. Once you do your intro, you can anchor to royalty free-background music, meaning that you won't have to pay copyright fees or royalties on the music.

There are plenty available; you just have to go to the right resources to buy it. There are limitations on how you can use the music. You want to read the fine print. Look for wording similar to this: "The music is allowed to be used for the following. . ." I found royalty-free music websites in the past that allow you to use the music for everything except podcasts. So, I repeat; make sure that you read the fine print on the royalty-free, and make sure that you are buying a royalty-free song that is, in fact, allowed to be used on podcasts.

One resource that has well over a million royalty-free songs is Audiojungle.net You can join an annual membership that allows you to buy songs a la carte. Audiojungle.net has several different options, but, once again, make sure that you read the fine print because each song or each resource is priced differently based on where you can use it. The last thing you want to do is pay $25 for a royalty-free song only to realize it cannot be on podcast.

In the past, I've gone to Google.com and searched for free royalty-free music. This provides a plethora of resources with royalty-free music. I know I've mentioned this twice before, but make sure you read the fine print.

Lastly, I wouldn't mess around with any of this music hunting or trying to buy background music. I would simply find an editor this is a one stop shop. They can even write your intro and outro script for you, record them with background music on it, and edit them for you.

Step 7: Create a Podcast Trailer (teaser for your show)

Creating a great podcast includes creating a great pod-cast trailer or teaser. The best way to do that is to create an audiogram of your intro and album art. Later in the book, I will go into details about how to create audiograms, but for now, know that this is something that can be created by any graphic designer or by using a platform like Headliner.app

Headliner allows you to create audiograms, podcast videos, and all kinds of other marketing collateral that you'll need in order to create your podcast. The Headliner app is completely free to use, but they do have a paid option. In my opinion, it's worth every penny upgrading to the Pro Edition, which is around $12 a month. They even have an option that allows you to paste the link to a specific podcast episode, and they automatically create audiograms for you and email them to you once a week, once a day, or one time (whatever you choose once your podcast is posted). I love audiograms, and audiograms are becoming more and more relevant within the podcast space because they are a great way to market your podcast. I'll go into more detail later in the book on what it would take to create an audiogram.

Let's talk about the creation of a podcast trailer. What you need to do is simply take the podcast cover art that you have created for your intro and outro, that's recorded either by your-self or someone else and tie it all of that together. You're creating a movie of sorts, but there's no video involved, there's an image, and there's audio, which makes it technically a video file being uploaded. You can use this to promote your show on social media. Post it, share it, and upload it. The trailer is uploaded to your podcast hosting account. You simply upload to Anchor, and it has an option to ask you if this is a trailer or an actual episode.

Step 8: Create episode 1 ROS (Run of Show)

Plan your work and work your plan. That's exactly what you need to do when creating your podcast and getting ready to launch your show. We've gone through 90% of the steps to create your podcast show, and it's now time to plan your very first episode. And when I say plan, I mean PLAN!

The next step in the process is a clean sheet of paper and a pen, or pencil (if that's how you roll), and write out a plan for your first episode. This is how you do it.

At the top of the page write the episode number and the name of the episode below. Then make 4 to 6 bullet points that you want to cover during the episode: topic to be discussed, things you want to discuss with your guest, things that contribute to the episode. That is what you are going to put in the blank space for the key points.

(Trust me on this, there's a method to the madness.)

Below the key points, leave a section, write notes and draw a line under it. This area is going to be where new things come up while planning your episode. It's important to remember that during the recording of the episode there are going to be several things you'll want to take notes on. You're going to have your show notes right in front of you, or at least you should. The last thing you want to do when recording a podcast episode or interview is to skip the planning and written notes. Do the planning; follow the plan.

NOTE: **Winging it is a terrible idea.**

Did I mention that winging it is a terrible idea? It totally is.

Most people are very nervous when recording their first episode, but if you take the time to plan out your episode and fill out the show notes page before your episode, you will be able to breathe easy, lower anxiety, and calm your nerves while recording your podcast episode.

After you've completely shown up, and you have planned out your first episode, you will now have your entire show in front of you on a sheet of paper. Do not use more than one sheet of paper. If you need more space to write, turn your one page over and write additional notes on the back, but don't overload yourself with information. If you fill out any more than one piece of paper, you're going to have a tremendous amount of information that you intend to cover, but never will do because of the time restraints.

Time flies when you're having fun, but I would like to also say that time flies when you're recording a podcast, especially when you're interviewing someone. An hour feels like around fifteen minutes. When you're recording your episode, drape a shirt or something else on the chair in front of you and speak to it as you would a guest.

Putting time stamps next to each key point reminds you that you're only going to talk about that point for a specific amount of time.

Make sure all of your guest's information is in the notes area if you're going to be interviewing someone. You want to be able to let your listeners know where they can contact and get in touch on the show.

Also, the enticing draw is for people to be interested in being on your podcast, but the very fact that you're talking about them and you're also promoting what they do and what their brand, service, or product is all about should be reason enough for them to be excited to be on your show.

Podcasting should be a win-win situation. You book compelling, creative interviews and content, and the interviewee gets additional exposure by being on your show. Even if your show is brand new, you're taking the time to talk with someone else, and that alone is sufficient reason for that someone to want to be on your show.

In later chapters in this book I'm going to go into detail about how to interview someone. Yes, there is an art to it, and I'm going to cover what I believe is the best strategy for an interview.

I'll give you a little hint: it has to do with Larry King. More later.

Step 9: Record Your First Episode

The next step in the podcast launch process is, you guessed it, the recording! The moment we've all been waiting for, ladies and gentlemen, children of all ages.

As I mentioned above, it's important to understand that you don't have to overcomplicate the process of recording your podcast episode. Seriously, this can be done on an iPhone 6, and it doesn't require a microphone.

When you're ready to record, grab the show notes that you've completed for episode one and press the record button! Time to verbally create what you have drawn out.

Step 10: Edit Your Episode

This could be the part of the Podcast Launch process that frustrates you. I'm forewarning you, podcast editing, or audio editing of any sort, is no fun in my book. That's why I <u>strongly</u> recommend that you find an audio editor to edit your podcast episode. As I mentioned before, there is a plethora of audio editors available on freelancer websites. I'll add links to those later on. There's no reason to frustrate yourself or add additional work to the podcast production process by attempting to turn into a podcast editor. You should be focused on one thing and that is your podcast recording, creating content, interviewing people, and growing your show through content. I speak from experience; trying to figure out how to edit a Podcast only leads to frustration. Now, if you're one of those people who like to figure things out like video editing or audio editing, well then, go nuts, knock yourself out. Heck, you may end up liking it.

You will find that the more that you're able to delegate to the podcast launch process, the easier the launch will become. I'm a firm believer in finding people who like to do the things that you do not like to do. It improves production and enables you to do what you do best; create podcasts.

If you want to try your hand at editing your podcast, you can do that with Anchor.FM, because with it you can create your intro, throw your episode in, throw your outro in, and the episode is edited. You can also use platforms and software like Garage Band or Audacity. These are both audio software that will allow you to put your episode together. This is not impossible; I've used these apps many times before. I just choose to not continue using them as I can hire someone to get it done for me.

These platforms allow you to literally drag and drop files into the software and arrange them in the order that you want them in order to edit and produce your entire podcast episode. If you're using Garage Band because you're a Mac user or Audacity because you're a PC user, you would open the application up and create a new project. The first file that you would drag or upload into the software would be your intro. Next, it would be your podcast episode, followed by the outro. There's a lot of dragging and dropping involved, but it's not impossible to figure out. As I said, I've done it, but I prefer to hire someone else to do it for me.

As I mentioned earlier, if you would like to do it yourself, I would highly suggest using Anchor when you're first starting your podcast. Anchor will allow you to create your intro, create your outro, record your episode, and add musical transitions. It's a different type of dragging and dropping in Anchor, as it's extremely simplified. You can always move away from Anchor to another podcast app if you choose, but get the rhythm, the mechanics, the basics, the foundation laid out and built out before trying to over complicate things that don't need to be complicated at all.

Podcast editing does not need to be difficult. The goal is to tie all of the components of your show together, the intro, the episode, and the outro, to make sure that the audio is adjusted accordingly, that you sound professional, and that everything is lined up the way that it should be.

Done is better than perfect when it comes to podcast editing, but the podcast editing process is not difficult. You can do it yourself. You can hire someone. Just get it done.

Step 11: Sign Up for Podcast Hosting

If you've completed the previous 10 steps, then you should be ready to upload your podcast episode. If you're going to use a platform like Anchor.FM when you're first getting started, GREAT! I recommend that for beginners, you can always move away later, then you're going to need to sign up for podcast hosting. There are several different options available for podcast hosting. A perk from Anchor.FM is that they give you free podcast hosting as part of the free platform; however, many seasoned podcasters would frown on Anchor.FM long-term and recommend that you sign up with a podcast host.

These are the top podcast hosting companies:

- SimpleCast
- Buzzsprout
- Libsyn
- Anchor.FM

These platforms will run you anywhere from $3 to $50 a month, depending on what you need, as far as a hosting platform is concerned.

At PodcastLaunchLab, we use SimpleCast.com for the ease of uploading a podcast episode, but more importantly, because we have our podcast distributed to multiple platforms like YouTube, SoundCloud, Spotify, iTunes, iHeartRadio, Stitcher, TuneIn Radio, and several more.

The goal of the podcast host is not only to host your audio files so they have somewhere to live, but also to provide you with distribution. Most podcast hosts will provide you with a podcast website as part of your hosting plan. Having a podcast website with your podcast is one less thing that you have to deal with in launching your podcast. Some people like to build a separate website just for the podcast, but I think it's redundant if your podcast host gives you a free website as part of your hosting plan.

Most of the platforms that I mentioned above are very easy to use, and if you get caught up and are confused about anything, they all have help resources in customer service available to walk you through the process of making sure that you get your podcast episode uploaded. If you want an example of what it's like to upload a podcast episode, it's very comparable to uploading a video to YouTube, except you're uploading an audio file instead of a video file.

When you upload the audio file, you put the title of the file, you put the description, which is from your show notes, and any keywords for relevant information, such as episode number and your podcast website. Of all these, the description part is the most important. I will get to that in the next step of uploading your podcast episode.

Don't over complicate the process of choosing a podcast host if you don't know which one to choose, because they all look the same. Go with the one that you feel resonates the most with you.

Step 12: Upload Your Episode

After you've locked down your podcast host, it's time to upload your first episode. Like I mentioned above, it's very comparable to uploading a video to YouTube. The only difference is that you're not uploading a video, you're uploading an audio file. When you sign up for your podcast host and go to upload your first episode, you're going to upload the audio file.

If there's a similar setup to what you would see on YouTube or Vimeo when uploading a video, the host will ask you what the title of the audio file is, then it's going to have a box for the description. This description is where all of the show notes that you wrote down on your piece of paper as your guide for your podcast episode will be converted into your show notes. This is very important because during the show, this is your point of reference; you'll say you'll be able to reach out to Sally because her website will be in the show notes.

The best part about a podcast is that once you upload one episode, it gets distributed to multiple platforms. You don't have to upload it to multiple platforms individually, which would take you forever. That's the goal of having a podcast host with distribution options; you have the opportunity to upload one file and have it distributed to over 15 or more different distribution platforms.

The syndication and distribution happen through what's called an RSS feed. The RSS stands for Really Simple Syndication. To break it down even more simply, you upload one file to one platform, and that platform distributes that piece of content to multiple distribution channels via your RSS feed. Every hosting account comes with an RSS feed; that's exactly how your podcast gets distributed. If you do everything manually as far as uploading a Podcast Episode to your podcast host and then submitting your show to multiple distribution platforms, each platform will require an RSS feed to be submitted on their platform so that they can approve your show to be within their network. Once that process is done, then every time a new episode is uploaded to your podcast host, it is distributed to all of the other distribution channels that you signed up for.

You will never upload an episode directly to any distribution platform other than your podcast host, and your podcast host technically is not a distribution platform. They are there to do two things: host your podcast and distribute it as requested.

Step 13: Market Your Podcast and TELL PEOPLE ABOUT IT!

If you made it to this step, congratulations! You are officially a podcaster. That means you've gone through each step that I mentioned above and have been able to create your show and produce your first episode and upload and post it. That's quite the accomplishment.

Now it's time to tell people about your show. Now it's time to market your show and to spread the word.

Here are a few ways to do that:

- Run a Facebook ad promoting your podcast Facebook page.

- Post album art or cover art on Instagram and promote the post.

- Send an email to your contacts list promoting the podcast, encouraging people to download it and subscribe to the show.

- Create an audiogram with Headliner.app and post an audiogram on social media.

- Be a guest on other podcast shows that are relevant to your brand and what you do. This is a phenomenal opportunity not only to promote your brand but also to promote your podcast.

- Tap into your existing community network of people. People want to help, but they just don't know where to help, so reach out. The worst that you're going to hear is no, but chances are the answer will be yes.

- Pinterest is another incredible platform to promote your podcast. You can upload a trailer, an audiogram, or your podcast cover art, or whatever marketing image that you created on Canva with the title of the episode with a short description and a duster Destination URL when you post the Pinterest pin. Pinterest gets a tremendous amount of traffic on a monthly basis, and if your content is relevant, you're going to be able to leverage the traffic to get people to check out your show.

Step 14: REPEAT

I wanted to make sure I was as thorough as possible with helping you understand the precise process that we've done at the PodcastLaunchLab.com since I started podcasting back in 2011. This is the exact process that you should follow. You will not fail if you use this process, and you just follow the steps I've created. There could be additional steps that you add into that process because you want to pay a little bit more attention to detail, and if that is the case, by all means, go nuts!

The important part here is that you actually launch your podcast.

Procrastination rarely pays off, so if you have gone through the steps and you're confident that you can complete them, well then, it's time to finally launch your podcast.

The time is NOW! Not tomorrow, not next week, not next year, NOW!

You're going to hear me say this several times throughout the book, but this time next year, you will be so happy that you've committed to starting your podcast, stuck with it, and now you have your own podcast show.

*Sidenote - A tremendous amount of FREE resources are available pertaining to what I mentioned above on my YouTube.com/PodcastLaunchLab channel)

Chapter 6
Market Your Podcast

There was never a mention of "easy," ever.

It has been said that anything worth doing is not going to be easy. Then again, if it were that easy everyone would be doing it, right? We've heard such quotes, slogans, and adages for as long as we can remember. The reason that we've heard them is because they're true.

I firmly believe that anything worth having is not going to be easy to obtain, but the payoff of getting to where you want to go is worth the path.

∫

Starting a podcast is not an easy venture, at all. But it's not impossible, and it's only as difficult as you make it. The biggest thing is to stay focused on your WHY and your vision for starting a podcast. When you're focused on doing something that you're passionate and excited about, the "work" tends to appear easy. Of course, that's an illusion that we develop based on the project that we are working on.

You can do the same thing with your podcast that you will someday monetize, and then the "work" will appear and feel easy. So what do you do when that happens? You go with it! You absolutely run with it! You take the momentum you have built and leverage it to complete the mission that you originally set out on: starting a podcast.

Next, we're going to talk about marketing your podcast, another venture that's not so easy. But again, if it was that easy, everyone would be doing it, and you would have a lot of competition within the podcasting space on what you do. What's critical is getting ahead of the game, getting ahead of your competition, figuring it out, and doing it before anyone else does. When I say anyone, I mean your present or future competition.

Marketing your podcast has to be done in a very creative way. Marketing a piece of audio isn't the easiest task, but then again, you didn't expect it to be easy, right?

In this chapter, I'm going to teach you to better understand the best practices for marketing your podcast. They're not the only ways to market your podcast, but they're the ones that I found to be the most effective, at least for now, as podcasting continues to evolve. These ideas are based on mainstream sources of consuming audio content.

So, for now, let's do our best to forget about easy, and just do the work. Stay committed to keeping your word to yourself on starting a podcast.

Oh, and don't ever forget, there was never a mention of easy.

Create Content to Market Your Show

Your podcast is a piece of audio, which makes it a little more difficult to market online than a video. Your podcast cover art that we talked about in the earlier chapters is vital to the branding of your show because it is essentially your show logo.

That logo could be used as collateral in a lot of your marketing efforts if you are willing to get creative by creating things like audiograms. Audiograms, like I briefly mentioned before, are a static image with audio put on top of it and saved as a movie. I'm sure you've seen them before online. They look like a movie, but they also look like a still image. They may have some squiggly looking lines to make it appear as it is something to promote an audio clip. That, my friends, is called an audiogram. They are great ways to be able to get the word out and market your podcast and pique people's interest.

People listen to 30 or 60-second audio clips that you put on top of an image. I like to use my podcast cover art as that image, and I like to go through the podcast episode and find one key nugget of information that is marketable. Something that someone is going to hear and say, "I want to listen to that episode." If I'm marketing the audiogram on Instagram, unless I'm putting it in my stories where I encourage people to swipe up to click on the link and go to my podcast website, I usually post the Audiogram with a link for people to subscribe to my podcast.

Post on Facebook, LinkedIn, Pinterest, or other sites that allow links, and post your audiogram, say something about it, and then put a call to action with your podcast website which gives people the opportunity to go listen, subscribe, wherever they choose. Do not be shy about giving them the opportunity to subscribe wherever they like.

As technology continues to evolve, it will evolve for podcasting, I'm sure there will be new, innovative technology and solutions to help us market podcasts more easily, but for now, we have images, audiograms, and the link directly to our podcast in order to encourage people to subscribe to it.

Audiograms 101

I mentioned this several times before, but an audiogram is a phenomenal way to market your podcast. You can post them on YouTube, Facebook, LinkedIn, and Instagram with a call to action to subscribe to your podcast or listen to this specific episode. On Instagram, we're talking about utilizing this as a promotional piece of content to direct people to download your podcast and listen to the episode by clicking on the link in your bio.

Other platforms like Facebook and LinkedIn that allow links are a lot easier for you to post audiograms on, as you can just post the audiogram with the link either in the comments below or within the post. Some would argue that putting a link in a Facebook or LinkedIn post decreases the engagement, but I've seen it work both ways. Adding a link to the post increases engagement; adding a link to the post decreases engagement.

Before I found out about software like Headliner or Kapwing. com, I would just get creative on my own. I created my own audiograms.

I would do that by opening up iMovie, dragging and dropping a one minute audio clip from my podcast into iMovie and an image or my cover art for my podcast and then saving the file as a movie. That worked pretty well for a while, but audiograms have advanced and improved. I wanted things like "Subscribe on Spotify or iHeartRadio." I wanted to have those icons on my cover art and audiograms, and I also wanted the squiggly lines that made it evident that this was a piece of content marketing an audio product like a podcast.

As I continued to do my research to find a solution, I stumbled upon a couple of different platforms that forever changed how I would create audiograms for my own podcast in addition to the podcast of the shows we launched here at the PodcastLaunchLab.com.

The first platform that I found was Headliner. This app is great web-based software that allows you to create audiograms automatically and custom based on what you create within the Headliner app. The most exciting thing about Headliner is that they have an automated solution. You can type in a link to your podcast episodes in and Headliner will find your show. Then it walks you through a series of steps to create an audiogram template.

This audiogram template within Headliner asks you a series of questions. What size do you want the audiogram to be? How long do you want the audiogram to be? How many times do you want Headliner to automatically send you these audiograms? One time only, once a week, every day? This saves you a lot of time having to sit down and create audiograms for each podcast episode that you have. Creating one is not that difficult, but having to do every time can me time-consuming.

Headliner eliminates all of that, especially if you use their automated podcast audiogram solution. They may call it automated podcast video. Your Audiograms are created with artificial intelligence. That means the Headliner software skims through your episode and assumes what the best 15-second, 32-second, 45-second, or 1-minute click will be. Once they figure this out, they email you the file (based on your preferences) every day, every other day, once a week, or just one time.

Now I know that you're probably thinking, "Well, if artificial intelligence creates the audiogram, what if it's the clip that I don't want?" Great question!

When Headliner sends you the email with your audiogram, it also gives you an option of going in and adjusting the specific clip so you can choose which clip is played. This is still easier than sitting down and creating a brand-new audiogram each and every time you want to create a piece of content. Headliner has all kinds of additional options: you can make your own audiograms from scratch. Using Headliner is very comparable to using a video or audio editor, but they make it significantly easier by having a everything within one easy-to-understand place. Trim and remove whatever features you don't want to create your audiogram.

Audiograms can be created as long as you have 30-second or 1-minute clips of your podcast and a marketable image. You simply login to headliner, drag and drop your audio, and you're off to the races, able to create podcast audiograms for your podcast.

This book is being written in 2020, and at this very moment, audiograms are simply one of the best ways to market your podcast. Headliner is a free solution that can help everything I've mentioned above become a reality for being able to create your own podcast audiograms.

Even if your show hasn't launched yet, an audiogram can be useful. You can take your podcast cover art and your podcast intro and create your first audiogram. This is a great way to get the word out even before the show launches. Go ahead and upload it; a teaser or trailer of sorts which allows people to go in and subscribe or download the teaser to get an idea of the show, anticipate your first episode, and get notifications, now that they're subscribed, when the show does go live.

Another great use of an audiogram before your show launches is to create what's called an extended teaser for the trailer. Or that's at least what I call it. You will record a 2 to 3-minute clip talking about your show and giving an extended introduction to the show. You'll create an audiogram with the intro, the teaser trailer that you recorded for two to three minutes, and then the outro. This can be shared on all social media and uploaded as a teaser or trailer to your podcast before the show launches so that people can get a better idea of what to expect when you launch.

Social Media Images for Marketing

Although podcasts aren't the easiest piece of social media content to promote, with platforms like Headliner and Canva.com, you can quickly become an audio editor, video editor, and graphic designer -- at least on an amateur level, that allows you to create the content that you need in order to market your podcast. Remember; podcasting is all audio, so you must come up with creative visual content to be able to market your podcast on social media.

One of the things that I like to do is record all of my podcast episodes on Zoom, which allows me to connect with my guest. I can see them and, most importantly, Zoom gives me the archived replay of the video and the audio of the interview that I've done. I then take screenshots of the interview and create some sort of branding or co-branding to be able to post on Instagram or Facebook, "Hey, I had Billy on the show last week, and we had a great time," tagging them and posting a picture.

You have to create as much content as you possibly can. Real time and after, in order to market your podcast episode. So, utilizing screenshots of the episode is totally cool. If you'd like to take the video replay and chop that up into 30-second or 1-minute pieces, you can create video memes. Video memes will have a title bar on the top, the video in the middle part, and some sort of image/branding on the bottom part, and the images.

Social Media Ads

Another great way to market your podcast episodes is by running ads for a very small dollar amount. Testing is the best route when using ads. People grossly underestimate the power of spending $1 per day to market their content.

If I told you that for $30, I would show your post to 5-10K people, would you do it?

Of course you would!

The best platforms to market your podcast and test out spending $1 or $2 a day are:

Facebook – Boost Your Post Ad

Instagram Ad – Promote Your Post

Pinterest.com – Promote Your Pin

All of these ad platforms make it VERY easy for you to setup and run an ad. You simply need to make sure you have an ad account set up on each platform, with a form of payment on file, and they will walk you through each step that it takes to run that ad, also known as "Boost The Post" or on Instagram "Promote The Post"

Your Email List

The email list for your business is another great way to promote your podcast. If you don't already have an email list, I would highly suggest starting one. Social media platforms are a great way to get the word out, but if you own your actual email list, you own the content and the list itself, this is far more powerful than posting something on social media, it's more personal.

Another great way to leverage email lists is by asking a business partner or associates that you work with if they'd be willing to get the word out for you. Ask them to send an email on your behalf, encouraging people to promote your podcast, and then ask them to be a guest on your podcast to talk about their business and their brand. This is another example of a win-win situation where you are helping someone and someone's helping you.

I would highly suggest creating a launch strategy to enroll your list into supporting you for the launch of your podcast. You can run some sort of contest. You don't have to give away cash, you can give away one of your products or services, offer a free consultation, or an Amazon Echo or Alexa or an iPad or whatever you decide is worth giving out for a prize for thanking people for helping you with your podcast launch. Deciding what that launch strategy is going to be is extremely important for you to do. The goal is to get people to subscribe to your podcast and download an episode out of the gate!

Be a Guest

Another great way to market your podcast is for you to be a guest on other people's podcasts. Search for podcasts that are within the vertical of work that you do, reach out to the show and offer to be a guest.

One great technique that I learned a few years ago is to go to LinkedIn.com and search for podcast hosts. You can search by state or by city. You'll find there a significant number of podcast hosts available on LinkedIn. All you need to do is connect with these people. Once you're connected with them, send them an email offering to be a guest on their show. If it's a fit, maybe you can be a guest on their show, and they can return the favor. This is a phenomenal way not only to promote your brand, but also to market your podcast. You are on someone else's podcast show, you talk about what you do, and you're bringing value to that show, and, most of the time, the podcast host is going to bring up and mention anything that you would like to promote or plug throughout that episode. That's a great opportunity to provide a call to action! Tell people to find you on Linkedin, follow you on Instagram, subscribe to your YouTube channel, and subscribe to your podcast. Now, you don't need to mention all of those, but definitely encourage people to connect with you on Linkedin and to subscribe to your podcast. It's an extremely effective way to get the word out, promoting your podcast using someone else's podcast is an extremely effective way to get the word out for free.

There are some services available that will offer to get you booked on other podcasts. I don't know of any offhand that I would be able to recommend, but I have heard within the industry that it is possible to hire someone to help you get booked on other podcasts. If that's the route that you would like to explore, try it out to see how it goes. Before venturing out to work with any of these companies that promise any sort of result, I would ask them which types of shows have those podcasters booked on as a guest. Do your research, know who you're working with. If it seems a little shady or uncertain, it probably is. BUYER BEWARE!

It's not difficult to reach out to someone these days via social media. It's a simple question, "Are you looking for new guests for your podcast?"

If the answer's "yes," continue the conversation. People produce a million podcasts right now, and that number is only going to continue to rise. As the podcast becomes more and more relevant, opportunities to guest on other podcasts will continue to increase. Be sure that you look for opportunities to be on other people's podcasts to talk about what you do and also talk about your podcast. In the beginning, you want to offer things like, "Hey, I'll be on your podcast, and you can be on mine." This is a great way to scratch each other's back and create a win-win solution. Maybe you can trade with other people whose podcasts are just getting started.

Marketing a Podcast isn't a Sometime Thing; it's an All-the-Time Thing.

Selling your podcast is something that you do all the time. I want to say every single day, but that might be a little excessive. At a bare minimum, every time you do an episode, create a couple of pieces of content and share it. It even may become useful long after the particular episode is released. In fact, six, seven, eight months from now, a year from now, two years, a lot of it can be repurposed. You can do great things like turn a podcast into a book, turn it into video content, etc.

Marketing Your Podcast Will Get People Through the Door. Branding Your Podcast Will Keep Them There.

Marketing your podcast is like a game of chess. You make little moves every single day that eventually converge into big moves. You start with smaller interview opportunities, and then you go on to bigger interview opportunities. You go from 500 downloads to 5,000 downloads then 25,000 downloads, and the show grows into something bigger than you would ever have imagined. But it takes persistence and consistency to get there. Rome wasn't built in a day, and neither will your podcast.

There's no magical time frame from starting a podcast to when it's going to become successful; it'll happen when it happens. But I can tell you that the process of your podcast becoming more and more relevant and popular is a direct reflection on the amount of effort you've contributed to actually staying with recording new episodes, promoting new episodes, and growing your podcast.

Podcasting is comparable to placing a billboard in the middle of the woods. Unless you promote it and tell people about it, no one is ever going to hear about it. Promoting your podcast is your job and your team's job, no one else's. If you don't care enough to do the marketing, no one else will care. That's why it's a must that you not only remain consistent with creating content for your podcast, but also remain consistent with creating content for marketing your podcast consistently.

Until some new technology hits the market, what I have taught you above are some practical ways to be able to market your podcast and spread the word for every episode that you're creating. I hope that you're taking a little bit more than just that from the chapter, as I've added some additional insight based on my personal experience of marketing my podcast. Remember that marketing your podcast and being consistent with it is the magic ticket and an almost sure way to be certain that you're spreading the word so that people know about your podcast, subscribe to your podcast, and become part of your podcast ecosystem.

Chapter 7
Podcast Interviews:
The Lifeblood of Your Show

One of the most important aspects of your podcast will be the interviews conducted on it. It's very rare that there is just one person talking the entire time on a podcast, unless you have something very interesting to share and you already have existing credibility and an existing community. The ability to fill time and space with just yourself is incredibly challenging. I do not recommend going that route in the very beginning. The only time that I suggest going solo on the podcast may be in episode 1 when the show host is launching the podcast in order to cast the vision for the show and help people better understand what to expect as the show unfolds.

The goal of your podcast is to feature other people doing other things. One reason for having guests is building relationships. Relationships have always and will always help us grow both personally and professionally. Having a guest visit your podcast and interviewing them is a phenomenal way to build a relationship with them. You're having a conversation with your guest for an extended amount of time, so, by default, you're building rapport, which enhances and establishes a relationship with them.

If you've never interviewed anyone on your podcast before, that's what this chapter is all about. I get questions all the time about how to conduct a proper interview on a podcast. How do you interview someone? What questions do you ask? How much should I be talking?

Interviewing guests increases your credibility and allows you to make and build new connections with people you want connections with. Interviewing also allows your audience to see inside someone else's world, rather than just the information you talked about on your podcast.

Your first interview should start during your second or third episode. There are no rules; it's entirely up to you. Sometimes we have students at the PodcastLaunchLab.com who want to do their first couple of episodes solo to explain what the podcast and your products will feature.

We call those first segments pillar episodes. It's an opportunity to cast your vision for the show and help people better understand what to expect moving forward. The pillar episodes prepare listeners for entering into the interview series. I recommend no more than one or two episodes by yourself, and then move right to the interview model for subsequent episodes of your podcast into your business. I understand you might not own a sales training company, but what kind of business and brand do you have? What kind of audience are you targeting? Opportunities are out there in the marketplace, and you can use a similar model in your podcast strategy.

Countless times, I have had a guest on my podcast show who has awakened me to new concepts.

Sometimes they have a way bigger following than I, yet they don't have a podcast. I ask them a simple question: "When are you starting your podcast?" I always encourage them to give a second thought to the idea of starting a podcast. They usually quickly say, "You know, I probably should!" To which I reply, "You absolutely should, and it would be my distinct pleasure to help you make that a reality. We should have another conversation after the interview."

9 times out of 10, they're all over the idea and down for that second conversation. Unlike most prospects for my product, I know a couple things about them. Number one, they're really smart, number two, they're doing better things than I am at the moment. Number three, they've gone a little bit further than I have, and number four, they're successful, so I know they can afford me.

The example I gave above should be enough encouragement for you to go, "Wait a second, maybe I could do something like that." FYI, you totally can!

Be on Other Podcast Shows.

Now, having guests on your show is great, a big part of your podcast, and it should be; developing your relationships with people, having them on your podcast telling their story, and providing value to your audience through someone else's valuable information. That's called a win-win. This strategy is great, but in addition to this, a flip-side strategy involves you being on other people's podcasts. The goal of this strategy is to make a new connection with someone who has a podcast, but more importantly to bring your knowledge and expertise to their show. During that process, they always ask the best way their audience can connect with you. They'll ask about your podcast and anything else you have going on. Being on other people's podcasts is a phenomenal opportunity for you to not only market yourself as a personal brand, but also the opportunity to market your podcast or your YouTube channel.

Sometimes you can even double dip: find someone that needs a guest on their show pertaining to what you do, and then you can have them on your show as a guest. You scratch their back, they scratch your back, and everyone wins.

In addition to the benefit of your providing valuable infor-mation to another podcast and connecting you with other podcasters, being a guest on other people's podcast allows you to see things from the other side of the equation because you are the guest now. Not a lot of work and logistics go into you being a guest other than making sure you have the date and time on your calendar (correctly) and then actually doing the interview. Another difference is that you're not the one asking the questions; someone else is asking you questions, someone else is productively picking your brain through a podcast interview. I get excited about both sides of the process. Of course, hosting a podcast -- asking all the questions, but being a guest on other podcasts is all kinds of fun in my opinion.

People you should interview

Not everyone is a fit for your show or for you to interview them. I constantly preach to our students at the PodcastLaunchLab. com that you want to find people who are smarter than you, doing better and cooler things than you, who are more successful than you. You obviously want to find individuals who have an interesting story. Stories make emotional connections with your listeners that helps them stick around long-term. I want to provide value on my podcast, sure, but people also want to relate to the content that you provide to them. When you strategically identify your guests to find out if there is a fit to interview them, you're looking for people who are smarter than you. I'm reminded of the quote, "if you're the smartest one in the room, you're probably in the wrong room."

The same applies with podcast interviews. In my opinion, if you have people on your show who are smarter than you and have been more successful than you, then you have an opportunity to be mentored. You have an opportunity to learn from them. You have an opportunity to pick their brain in a very constructive way, while providing extremely valuable information and content to your audience. Besides that, if they're cooler than you, having them on your podcast makes you cool; I'm totally kidding about the last part, kind of.

I told the story of my buddy who owns the sales training company here in Miami above. I want to go back to that for a minute because it has to do with the point that I'm making concerning people whom you should interview on your podcast. I just finished telling you that your guests should be smarter than you are and doing bigger things have you have done. You can learn from them and get as much value as possible. First, though, you need to identify who these people are.

- Who is your ideal client?
- Who's your avatar?
- Who's your target market?

These are questions to ask yourself when you are seeking out new guests for your podcast. You want to be strategic. It's almost as if you're reaching out and prospecting, but you're not asking for a meeting or a sale, you're asking for someone to be on your podcast. People are more inclined to be on your podcast than they are to give you an appointment for a sales call. Why? Because they field a hundred sales calls a day. Ask me how many podcast interview requests they get. Chances are not a lot, especially in the corporate world. I believe that's all going to change in due time sooner rather than later, but for now I'm pretty sure your competition is not utilizing podcasting as a means of prospecting. Podcasting as a means of prospecting? What does that even mean? That means that you're seeking and identifying strategic people who are going to bring valuable content to your show.

Now this is only one strategy that I shared with you pertaining to prospecting by getting people to be interviewed on your show. There's not always a sales opportunity for a future business opportunity with the interview that you're going to be conducting. It may be somebody you really admire, really like their work, resonate with their story, and you just want to have a conversation with them and let them tell their story on your podcast.

There are really no rules pertaining to podcast interviews. I just strongly believe that you should be very strategic because you are taking time to create content, interview someone, and have them on your podcast. You always want to keep the listener in mind. As long as your content is valuable pertaining to the person that you're interviewing, I strongly believe that it's still time well spent.

Build Relationships

As I close this chapter out, I want to drive home the point that being able to establish a strategic podcast interview guest is a phenomenal opportunity for you to build relationships. You're probably already focused on building relationships for your brand and your business, as they are the lifeblood of your business and your brand. I firmly believe that having guests on your podcast allows you to establish new relationships and strengthen existing ones. The unknown of the podcast world, as far as opportunities is concerned, is the most exciting part to me. You simply never know what's going to happen. You sit down, have a conversation, and you see where it goes. More times than not, there's some form of benefit being established by both parties simply by sitting down and having a conversation on your podcast.

I decided to write this chapter specifically about podcast interviews because I get feedback from PodcastLaunchLab. com students and people within my community asking me, "Sebastian, how do I conduct a podcast interview?" Well, I have no problem explaining how to conduct a podcast interview, and I want to drive home the point of the opportunity at hand for you to be able to build relationships and establish new connections by interviewing people on your podcast.

How to Interview a Guest

There is no right or wrong way to interview someone on your podcast; after all, it is your podcast. However, if you are talking more than your guest is talking, that is a problem. Like the old saying goes, if you think you're talking too much, you are. Keep that in mind when interviewing people on your podcast.

I'll never forget learning from the legendary Larry King about his 80/20 rule when interviewing people. King interviewed world leaders, celebrities, and regular people alike for decades, and he was at the top of his field. Your guest should be talking 80% of the time, and you should speak no more than 20% of the time. King also encourages using words like "why" to be able to help your guests expand on exactly what they're talking about on your podcast interview.

In the beginning of the episode, you can give a short introduction welcoming listeners to your show. After your introduction, you'll explain details about your guests and then introduce your guest. This always should be a very enthusiastic part of the show. If you're not excited, how in the world are your listeners going to get excited? Yes, even through audio, people can pick up on whether or not you're enthusiastic, regardless of your personality.

Remember not to talk over your guest, and try not to laugh and chime in like you want to respond to each and every word that comes out of their mouth. That's annoying, and it's rude. Let your guests do what they're there to do: talk, provide value, and answer the questions you're asking them on your podcast.

If you don't know your podcast guest well, it's always good to send them a list of proposed questions that you'd like to ask them. Sometimes even do a follow up call to make sure everybody's on the same page. I like to ask my guests if there's anything that's off limits. I like to make my interviews like a conversation, but I like to dig deep when I'm interviewing a guest, and I want to know whether the guest has any boundaries. Boundaries are totally fine, as I don't want to make my guests feel uncomfortable. I want to stay in line with what they want to discuss while pushing the boundaries as much as possible.

Just remember, you're not Howard Stern, and you probably never will be. Pushing boundaries, especially just to see what will happen, rarely pays off... unless of course you are Howard Stern, and that hasn't always paid off for him either.

In Conclusion

I hope this chapter has brought some clarity to you as far as the power of podcast interviews. Remember, it's not just about your having strategic people on your podcast, but also about you being on other people's podcast to provide value and to promote your brand, your business, and, most importantly, your podcast content. Every interviewer has a personal style.

I gave a few short thoughts on an entry-level thought process to interview someone. Some of you may not have high energy, some of you may be laid back. I encourage you to dig a little deeper and find out what you can do to give 110% and show up with as much enthusiasm as possible.

Remember, your guest is going to feed off your enthusiasm and the energy that you give to interviewing them, and your audience is also going to feed off your enthusiasm and energy.

Remember, if you're not excited, and your guest is not excited, what in the world are your listeners going to feel like? You constantly need to keep in mind how your listeners are going to respond. Your podcast is all about your listeners. Your podcast has nothing to do with you and nothing to do with the guest that you interview. But it has everything to do with the people who are listening in, consuming, and sharing your podcast and guest.

You don't need to be a seasoned pro to conduct a podcast interview. If you follow the simple steps that I provided above, you should be off to a great start interviewing people and creating as much value as possible, building relationships, establishing rapport, and making new connections with guests you have on every podcast episode.

One good strategy is using a podcast interview to develop a relationship and then converting the relationship to business. Or by having guests on your show simply because they've got a great story. There may be no further opportunity for business or commerce, but the very fact that these interesting guests were on your show provides a tremendous amount of value for your podcast.

When you interview somebody who has more success than you have and has done more things than you have, usually they have built a larger network than you have. Almost by default, your guest shares with his or her contacts that they were on your podcast. Why? Because everyone likes to talk about themselves, and being interviewed by you on your podcast is doing just that. So if you have John Doe on your show, and John Doe has a million followers, and you send John Doe a link or image for the podcast episode to share with his network and they tag you, that, by default, is marketing and branding your podcast simply by having someone else on your podcast who has a bigger following.

One last thing I would recommend regarding people that you have on your podcast: I would have them agree, prior to the interview, that they will share the episode that they're on. It takes a half a minute to share a podcast episode. It's best to go in yourself and create a marketing flyer in Canva and provide a direct link to your podcast show. You can even go as far as writing the copy for the post. This will give them the opportunity to take that image and the copy you've written and the link to your podcast show and drop an email out to their list, sharing the episode in that information and content on LinkedIn, Facebook, Twitter, and every other social media platform out there.

Most of the time, people like to be told what to do, so ask them, "Hey, listen, I'm going to have you on my podcast show. After I interview you, would you mind sharing the episode link? I'm going to provide you with a marketing image, the copy for the post, and a link directly to the podcast episode.

This way, it will make it extremely easy for you to be able to copy paste and share to your network. Can you commit to sharing the episode that you're going to be on?" Get a commitment from them prior to the interview. Too many times before, I've asked very nonchalantly if they would share the podcast episode they were on. They casually give me a yes, and then nothing ever gets shared.

More than just asking them to commit to sharing the podcast episode, give them a reason why it's important to you. Usually when people make an emotional connection to you, your request will be honored. Say something like, "Hey, would you mind sharing my podcast episode that you were on? It's really important for me to make sure your network provides as much value as possible, and I think you can accomplish that by sharing my podcast episode."

If you follow the steps I've outlined in this chapter, you will be well on your way to becoming a total rockstar at interviewing people!

Chapter 8
Monetize Your Podcast

Not so fast!

It's pretty common for me to have conversations with people about starting a podcast. The first thing they want to talk about is how they can make money with a podcast. While having a monetization strategy in place is smart, when you first start your podcast, monetizing it is not a priority. There are enough challenges to go into the launch of the podcast and the podcast process and ongoing process by themselves. Trying to figure out how you're going to monetize a show with no listeners makes zero sense. My response to those individuals is, not so fast. You must build it. Once you've built it, then you can get creative and figure out a way to find strategic opportunities to monetize your show.

Is it easy to monetize a podcast? My answer to that question is, yes and no. In this chapter, I explain exactly what it takes to arrive at a place where it's time to monetize your podcast.

You have to build it first.

You have to create the show, launch the show, and make sure the show continues. This includes continuing to create new content, to record new episodes, to conduct new interviews, and to build your online community, whatever that may look like. What I mean by an online community is a Facebook group or a LinkedIn group or your email list or a community of people who are currently engaged with what you do.

Maybe these people came to you through means of your podcast or maybe they were already in the community and learned about your podcast. They all can still become fans. It doesn't matter how you go about building your community; only you know what's best for you. But you must build something to monetize anything.

Advertisers and sponsors want to see and know a few facts when exploring opportunities. They want to know

- How big is your community network?
- How many downloads do you have on your podcast on a monthly basis?
- What kind of traffic is your podcast website seeing?
- What type of following do you have individually?
- What type of following does the show have?

These are all vital things that any advertiser, sponsor, or prospect looking to form a strategic, revenue-generating model with you would want to know. The only way these statistics are generated is to actually build your podcast and distribute it. I talked a lot about focusing on the development launch and ongoing success of the show because it is extremely important. Without all of those components, there is no monetizing the show.

If you're reading this right now, you might be thinking, "I've already got a community when I launch my podcast," or "When I launched my podcast, it was an instant success because my community is extremely responsive to the content that I create and send out to them."

You may experience a launch that had several thousand downloads right out of the gate, a highly engaged community and people raving about the show.

If this is the case, you are a unique example of what can take place when you launch a podcast when you've already got authority within the marketplace. Does this mean you can expedite the process of monetizing your show? Probably. Why? Because you've already got the numbers to prove exactly what you have to offer pertaining to your podcast and what you can do to expose the sponsor or brand.

Please understand, this is extremely rare unless you're a celebrity or an existing person of authority with a huge community. The average person starting a podcast is starting from scratch. I try to be responsibly transparent when explaining this process to you, as I don't want to get your hopes up. But at the same time, I don't want you to get discouraged, thinking that it takes forever to monetize your podcast. I just want to drive home the point that it's extremely important to stay focused on the development, the launch, and the ongoing success of the show, without; there will be no show or monetization.

Now I will give you some tactical ideas that you can utilize once the show has started to grow, and your community, so they arrive at whatever space you think you should be at to start going after advertisers, sponsors, and strategic revenue-generating opportunities for your podcast. These are just some things that I've come up with that I've seen happen and that seem to work within the marketplace and within my own show too.

The best part about having your own podcast is that you call the shots, which means you make up the rules. There's no one telling you what you can or can't do, but you need to advertise your sponsors' revenue opportunities, what you sell, what you offer, and what you talk about. Those all remain completely in your control.

Best Practices That Work Effectively

1. **Sell Something** - This could be a coffee cup, this could be hand sanitizer, this could be a t-shirt, this could be bumper stickers. Whatever you choose to offer on

your podcast and sell your audience is entirely up to you. If they buy what you're offering, you monetize the show, even if it's $5.

2. **Affiliate Programs (Amazon)** - People often ask me what I recommend for a podcast microphone. I quickly send them to PodcastLaunchLab.com, and I tell them to click on my podcast equipment recommendations. That brings them directly to my Amazon store. If they click and buy something, I make a commission. I mention that constantly on my podcast and in my YouTube videos. Amazon would love to have you as an affiliate. They do require you to have a minimum sale of about $20 a month, but that's easy to do if you're constantly talking about something relevant, like what are my podcast equipment recommendations are. I want to show people and showcase what they are, and the people decide to buy them. I like to be compensated by the vendor, which happens to be Amazon.

You can do the same thing. Maybe you want to review specific products, and when you're reviewing them on your podcast, you send them to a direct link on your website, which just happens to be your Amazon store. Being transparent about your being an Amazon affiliate is totally cool with most people. People understand the branch of affiliate programs, in which other people talk about them, and when people buy from them specifically, because they are an affiliate, they are compensated accordingly. The customer doesn't pay any more for your earning a commission.

3. **Monthly and Weekly Advertisers and Sponsors** - Another great way to monetize your show is through advertisers and sponsors. This happens when they're willing to pay a specific dollar amount for a specific amount of exposure via the show. In this case, it's your podcast show. Podcast advertising is becoming more and more relevant, so agencies have ad budgets for brands to advertise on podcasts. They are willing to pay a specific cost per thousand impressions. They normally want to know how many downloads you have, how big the community is, so you really have to prove your stuff in order to lock down a big brand sponsor. It all comes down to how big your community is and how many people downloaded your show on a monthly basis. They want fresh and existing listeners.

They want to know that the show aligns with their brand. The days of just putting some loud car dealership advertisement on the radio while it talks over a DJ and plays the same song over and over again are over.

This is another scenario where you make up the rules. We're not talking about big brand advertisers. We're talking about strategic brands that align with your show, your message, and your story. If an advertiser is willing to pay you $100 a month for you to mention them for 15 seconds 4 times a month, how long is that going to take you to add to that your show. And how much were you making from an advertiser before that? These are all realistic things that you want to keep yourself in check with. Don't let your ego get in the way. You should take a close look at, and pay attention to, any dollar amount that makes sense that may move you forward and create an opportunity for advertisers and sponsors and your show.

If you're just getting started with your podcast, make this model of securing an advertiser sponsor for your show your goal. Build the show's focus on new content, focus on building new relationships, building your community, getting people to engage and download your podcast on a monthly basis. Know that the end goal is to build the show to a place that advertisers and sponsors are attracted to your content and they're knocking on your door versus the other way around.

Initially, chances are you're going to be the one doing all the knocking and talking. That's right, it's a little game of, "hey, look at me over here." You have to prove your worth. You have to show your stats, you have to show what you've done, and you have to create value for the advertiser and sponsor to be attracted to what you are offering, what's on the table pertaining to their advertising on your show.

4. Cost Per Acquisition Models - Another model has a little less friction pertaining to advertisers and sponsors, and that is the cost per acquisition model.

What it simply means is that you offer someone else's product or service by talking about it on your podcast, maybe even interviewing them about it. If people inquire and they buy the product, you're paid a commission. This is very comparable to the affiliate model that I mentioned above with the Amazon affiliate example.

Suppose that you're in a business that is related to snowboards, but you don't specifically sell snowboards. Rather, you offer a service for people who buy snowboards. You could have a snowboard manufacturer on your show talking extensively about the new line that's coming out this winter. If your listeners become highly engaged and interested in snowboarding, then you can send them to a specific place where they can purchase the products. Once they buy, you get a commission. This is a very smart model that almost everyone is open to because there is no risk upfront.

It's not unheard of for new podcasters to be more concerned about selling their own products than securing advertisers and sponsors, just for the simple fact you feel you can make more money and generate more revenue simply by selling your own products and services versus hunting down advertisers and sponsors that you have to prove your worth to. There's a lot of truth to that, and if you have a compelling product or service that you can talk about consistently, even if your show has just started, then why not offer those types of products and services to your audience? You keep control, you don't have to sell yourself constantly to your advertisers and sponsors, and it fits within your brand and helps you market your products or services that much better.

If you're just beginning, it doesn't matter if only two people listen to your show. Those two people could be interested in your product or service. If they're interested in your product or service, they're going to buy it, and if you have two listeners and they buy a product, guess what? You've monetized your podcast! There is no time frame for you being able to monetize your podcast. Yes, it can be done right out of the gate; I'm just saying that it's not very common. However, if you have an existing audience and a great product, service, or offer that people will resonate with, then by all means; offer it on your podcast and get someone to purchase it.

There's something to be said for maintaining control and not having to constantly prove yourself to advertisers and sponsors spending money on a monthly basis to gain exposure through your show. That old saying; there is no free lunch – it's true. No advertiser is going to simply take your word for it because you're cool, you have great content, and you have a million followers on Instagram. Your claims must have data behind them before prospective advertisers or sponsors will want to get exposure through your show by being able to resonate with your audience and hopefully convert them to customers and raving fans due to their advertising on and sponsoring of your show.

While you are selling your own products, you are getting advertisers and sponsors. Simply being involved with affiliate programs is a phenomenal way for you to monetize your podcast. Ultimately, the choices are yours as far as how you want to monetize. There are no rules when it comes to monetizing your podcast other than simply the ones that you create. You decide on the best fit for you.

I hope this chapter has brought some insight and understanding of what it takes to monetize your podcast. Don't rush into figuring out how you can make money the first, second, third, fourth day, or even third or fourth month. Focus on building the show, recording new episodes, creating new relationships, interviewing new people, building your network. Then get strategic about finding sponsors, advertisers, and revenue-generating models that make sense and are aligned with your show.

In my experience, I found that when you find brands and products that align with your show, it's less abrasive to your listeners. Why? Because they're actually interested in what the ad or the sponsor has to say because it's in line with the content of your show. It makes sense for sponsors and advertisers to get exposure on your show, because their audience is your listeners.

These are all great things to keep in mind when identifying advertisers, sponsors, and revenue-generating models for your podcast. Alignment is so important, specifically when it comes to people who are willing to spend money on your show. You want to make sure that those individuals are resonating with your audience, and your audience is resonating with them.

Chapter 9
Podcast Equipment:
You Only Need an iPhone

If I could sum this entire chapter up with one sentence, it would be, "You can do this with an iPhone." There's no need to overthink podcast equipment when you start a podcast. You have everything within your possession to start your show, which is simply your phone.

I'm an iPhone user, so I've never used an Android to start a podcast, but I do know for sure that the Anchor.FM app works on any type of smartphone. You can use any phone to record your podcast!

The iPhone has an incredible embedded tool called the Voice Memo.

In addition to that, iPhones have incredible microphones already built in. As long as you're in a quiet space, you can utilize the Voice Memo app with no microphone attached other than the one that comes with your iPhone. It's always advised to use the corded earbuds that are provided with each iPhone. Plugging them directly into your phone will replace the phone's internal microphone and use the headphone microphone.

There tends to be a little bit more filtering of sound, and the quality of your recording is slightly better with the earbud microphone. I share all these things with you so you know you have everything that you need in your smartphone.

If you can simply focus on creating the content that your show is going to be all about, and not get bogged down in logistics, you'll find it a lot easier to get going when you first start your podcast. Too many people worry they can't afford an expensive microphone or that they need a studio or they need everything to line up perfectly.

I'm here to tell you today, that if you're waiting for the stars to align when money ain't funny and all's right with the world, you're never going to start a podcast. Oh -- FYI, the stars are never going to align, and money will never be funny unless you have too much of it (or you're playing the game Monopoly).

So if you're reading this right now and it's starting to resonate with you that you don't have to go on to Amazon and

Google to find the best podcast mic for $50 and attempt to play audio engineer and choose podcast equipment, but rather just focus on recording and creating your show, you're going to find it a lot easier to begin the process of starting your podcast.

Get 10, 15, 20 shows under your belt first utilizing your iPhone, recording with the Anchor.FM app, using your voice recorder app. If you're an iPhone user, the GarageBand app comes on your iPhone.

You can record it within the GarageBand app if you want to get technical and fancy with recording your podcast on your iPhone and then edit it.

There are multiple options available simply with the device that you're currently holding in your hand. Anything above and beyond utilizing what you already have when starting a podcast is simply creating an additional barricade in between where you are and where you want to be pertaining to your podcast launching. Remember, too many people get bogged down in minute details instead of just focusing on being able to create a podcast and actually get the show off of the ground.

Crawl, Walk, Run, SPRINT!

In my opinion, podcast equipment is a crawl, walk, run, sprint process. In the paragraphs below, I explain what I mean by crawl-walk-run-sprint when pertaining to podcast equipment and exactly what you need. Again, did I mention you can do this with an iPhone?

Crawl: iPhone

Every single iPhone on the planet comes with a free application already on the phone called Voice Memo; it also comes with a pair of corded earbuds that plug into your iPhone. This is all the podcast equipment that you will need. You can utilize the Anchor.FM app to record directly from your phone; you can use the Voice Memo app to record; you can use a third-party voice recording app; or you can use GarageBand, another app that is available through the iPhone platform.

As far as Android users are concerned, the only advice I can give you is utilizing something comparable to the Voice Memo app (there are several Android equivalents) or utilizing Anchor, which is available on any type of smartphone. This is the simplest approach to creating content and recording your show.

You probably want to ask me about interviewing people on Zoom. Well, you're in luck, as Zoom has a capability to interview someone within their app and also record the podcast episode or the Zoom call that you're actually on. So there really is no challenge when it comes to creating content on your phone.

For beginners, I always recommend starting here, getting into the rhythm of creating content to record podcast episodes. But don't just assume that it's going to be easy if you have all the equipment in place and everything ready to go. It's going to be easy when you make it easy, when you create hacks and find ways to leverage what you already have to accomplish the goals that you want.

When you're starting a podcast, the goal is to record podcast episodes, to do podcast interviews, and create content for your podcast.

We're living in an incredible time where we hold this little piece of equipment in our hands and it gives us access to the world. It gives us the ability to create, and it breaks down barriers that we previously had to creating content. Never in a million years did you think you'd be holding a device in the year 2020 that would allow you to record a podcast show or a YouTube video or go live on a social media platform. If someone had told you this 20 years ago, you would have told them they were completely out of their tree.

The bottom line is; we're here, technology isn't going anywhere, and it's definitely not slowing down for any of us. Technology doesn't care about your feelings, technology is going to continue to move, it's going to continue to improve, and it's going to continue to take over the world, with or without you.

Walk: USB Mic

So, the walk part of this process would be if you actually want to invest in buying a podcast microphone, nothing extravagant, but something simple, something that would enable you to actually improve the sound quality of your podcast.

If that is the case, I would recommend utilizing a USB microphone. These are available online at Amazon, electronics stores, and Best Buy, for example. They'll run anywhere from $60 to $130, depending on which one you get. The best part about a USB mic is that you simply plug it into your computer, and it's usually plug and play. For example, if you open up Zoom for a Zoom call, Zoom's going to ask you which microphone you want to use.

If your USB microphone is currently plugged into your computer, you're able to utilize that microphone. The best part about USB microphones is that they are plug-and-play, and they take your voice and improve the quality of it. When I first started, I used the Logitech Headset mic and then upgraded to a Blue Snowball microphone, a USB mic that plugs directly into your computer. A Blue Snowball is a round mic that fits on the small stand it comes with, and that plugs into your computer via USB and improves the sound of your voice drastically. Although these are USB microphones, they take the sound of your voice and improve it so that you sound better when you're recording your podcast.

In addition to the Blue Snowball microphone, there's also a Blue Yeti microphone that'll run you anywhere from $120 to $150, depending on which one you choose. It works the same way as the Blue Snowball. It sits on a stand in front of you and plugs directly into your computer via USB. It doesn't matter if you podcast on GarageBand, Zoom, or any other voice recording software. Your computer will always recognize your USB microphone as long as it's plugged into your computer. In addition to these being very efficient for improving the quality of the sound of your voice. They're very efficient as they are powered by plugging them into the USB on your computer, or simply plug the microphone into your computer via USB.

There are several other types of USB microphones available, but as far as quality is concerned, you want to stick with a reputable brand. Yes, you may get lucky and find an aftermarket USB microphone that still sounds good, but if you're not familiar with the brand, chances are it's an off brand not made by a large manufacturer, and you're going to suffer pertaining to quality. I would stick with the Blue brand, either the Snowball, or the Yeti. Another reputable brand is Audio-Technica. They have a few USB microphones that operate the same way as the Blue microphones operate. You simply plug them into the USB outlet in your computer, and you're off to the races.

It doesn't matter which USB microphone you choose, but if you are investing in a microphone, invest in a quality microphone with a reputable brand that is known for making USB microphones. You will know that it's not going to become a problem down the road when it unexpectedly fails to work or it doesn't improve the overall sound of your voice. After all, that is the goal of having a USB microphone or upgrading your microphone.

Run: Scarlett Studio

When I really started to get serious about podcasting, I knew it was time to upgrade my existing USB microphone solution. I had a Blue Snowball, which I still have, and it still works great as a traveler or on the road mic.

I was on a cruise back in 2019, and I met a friend on board. He's a financial advisor in Nashville, Tennessee with a background in sound engineering. I'm frequently seen wearing my famous "podcasts SUCK (if you don't have one)" t-shirt that I came up with a few years back. And for good reason. Those t-shirts really trigger a conversation with people about podcasts, which was the goal. My new friend strongly advised me to upgrade my USB Mic. I'd already been thinking about doing it, I just didn't know which direction to go.

As our conversation continued, he was extremely adamant about my exploring an option of an upgraded microphone that would still give me the USB capability that plugs directly into my computer but also upgrades the microphone overall to improve my sound quality, but the difference is night and day. At first, I was extremely resistant because I was very comfortable with my USB microphone that I can plug directly into my computer. I'm a firm believer in not over-complicating the podcast recording process while still being able to capture and record episodes with quality. My buddy was not hearing any of that. He was convinced that I needed to upgrade my podcast microphone game, and he was going to show me exactly what to do and how to do that. He said that I needed to get a setup called the Scarlett 2i2 Studio, made by Focusrite. The set comes with a professional mic that plugs into a small receiver box via a traditional XLR microphone cable. Adjusting your volume lows, mids, and highs is a very simple process. That box will plug directly into your computer USB. So whether you record in GarageBand or whatever, they're going to ask what your microphone source is; you choose Scarlett Studio. I heard him out, and I saw how adamant and passionate he was about advising me. So I finally gave in -- well after the cruise, because he had followed up to make sure I had upgraded.

I was extremely pleased with the set-up because it was a complete upgrade of an actual microphone, not just a USB microphone to improve the sound of an actual condenser microphone that would plug into a receiver into my computer. This upgrade allowed me to improve my voice tone overall and make sure that I sound as professional as possible despite not using a professional microphone. My biggest concern was that I was going to be over complicating the process and getting bogged down in the logistics of microphones and equipment and buttons and things that I didn't want to be concerned about. I just wanted to focus on recording podcast episodes. That couldn't have been further from the way that it actually worked out. I was pleasantly surprised that the entire setup was less than $300. The box had two microphone outlets, and came with a microphone headset and a microphone cord. All I needed to do was plug everything in and I was ready to go. There were a few additional things to plug in, including an actual Blue Snowball microphone like I had before. At the end of the day, it was still the same process as far as being able to set up my podcast microphone. Go toPodcastLaunchLab.com, and look under my "podcast equipment recommendations" in the top menu. There you will find all of my favorite podcast equipment that I've used and that I recommend to my students.

I'm really glad that I met my buddy on that cruise ship that day, and I'm really glad that he strongly encouraged and refused to give up on upgrading my microphone game. I discovered the wonderful world of the FocusriteScarlett Studio microphone setup.

This is a phenomenal solution if you're looking for something for less than $300 but want a credible sound improvement for your podcast recording. I've given you several different tiers that you can utilize for being able to upgrade your podcast microphone game, and I have one more for you.

This setup served me well for at least a year and a half, and then when I opened the PodcastLaunchLab.com Studio, I was somewhat obligated to again upgrade my podcast micro-phone game. And that's exactly what I did.

Sprint: Rodecaster Pro + PodMics

I went from running to sprinting with my podcast upgrade game when I opened the PodcastLaunchLab.com Studio in January 2020. I opened the lab because I needed a multiple microphone solution, which is exactly what the Focusrite gives me. Don't get me wrong, if it's just you and another co-host, the Focusrite will serve you guys perfectly. You simply add an additional microphone. Any microphone works, but the Focusrite receiver box makes your voice sound more professional.

I kept hearing amazing things about the Rodecaster Pro. This system allows you to plug up to four microphones into it, four headset outlets into it, and preload sound effects. You simply press the button, and the sound effects play. In addition, it has Bluetooth capability. People can call your cell phone while you're recording, and you can patch that person into the podcast you're recording. And it connects directly to any computer via USB. In my mind, that was an absolute no-brainer of a solution that I absolutely needed in order to upgrade my brand new studio, and that's exactly what I did.

At the time, I was opening the podcast studio, and I decided to buy a Rodecaster Pro from Rode. The same company had created what they call their PodMic, a cost-effective solution to getting a high quality microphone bearing the same brand as the Rodecaster Pro that I had decided to buy for the studio. So I purchased two Rodecaster Pro mics and two Audio Technica headsets. This is a good point to talk about headsets in a second.

The Rodecaster Pro, in 2020 when I wrote this book, is $599. The cost of a PodMic is $99 if you want two mics, and for the Rodecaster Pro you're looking at around $800. Still not a ton of money to have a professional-grade podcasting board and professional-grade podcasting microphones.

You can see why I called this section Sprint. You may be thinking, I'm just starting my podcast and I can buy whatever type of microphone that I want to buy. It won't be a challenge for me to invest in the best right out of the gate. If that's you that I'm talking to, then by all means, go buy a couple of Rode PodMics, a Rodecaster Pro, and you will be off to the races.

As you can see, my whole thought process of crawl-walk-run-sprint when you are identifying podcast microphone solutions is all about three considerations: Number One, the quality of microphone that you're getting; Number Two, how much money you want to spend on your podcast microphone equipment solution; Number Three, how advanced you want to be when you first get started.

It doesn't matter to me where you get started, all the solutions that I've mentioned above are extremely effective for recording your podcast with the best quality and sound possible. In all fairness, I had to give you my opinion relative to different levels of podcast equipment that you can explore to find an option that is best for you. That's not for me to decide but for you to decide. Again, you can do this with an iPhone. The solutions mentioned above really are going to allow you to continue to up your podcast microphone game and improve the quality and sound of your podcast microphone. Allow me to reiterate one more time that any of these solutions that I have mentioned above are not required in order to record your podcast episode. Stay focused on recording your episodes, hosting interviews, creating content, building relationships. As the show continues to grow, you can swing for the fences and get the best podcast equipment, but in the beginning, there's no need to overdo it, overthink it, or do all kinds of unnecessary steps when you're first getting started.

I was going to write an entire section about headphones, but there's no need to do that. At the studio, we use Audio Technica ath m20x headphones that run about $59 a pair.

I utilize these because they're comfortable and they don't hurt my ears if I wear them for a long time. Purchasing studio headphones is not important, because you can use just about any pair of headphones these days when recording a podcast. If you go with the solution that I mentioned above with the Focusrite Scarlett Studio, they have a bundle that comes with a pair of headphones already. In fact, you can find several Blue Snowball and Blue Yeti bundles on Amazon that will send you a bundle as well that will include headphones, a microphone scissor desk arm, a pop filter, and of course a USB microphone. Amazon is full of all kinds of help.

The two main places that I buy podcast equipment from are sweetwater.com, and amazon.com when I'm making larger equipment purchases like a broadcaster pro and more expensive microphones. I love a brand like sweetwater.com, as they give you a dedicated sales rep who is educated on the products they offer. I can only guide you in the right direction. Oftentimes, sweetwater.com gives you whatever discounts are available. Those are things that are not available on Amazon.

I'll end this chapter exactly the way that I started it. You can record a podcast on your iPhone. Do not overthink this process. When you do that, you just create another layer of getting in your own way and moving yourself just that much further away from actually achieving your goal, which is recording your podcast episodes.

I've laid out these crawl-walk-run-sprint solutions above so you're not overthinking. You just want a solution that's right for you, and I wanted to share what my experience has been. I wanted to give you three different price points for podcast equipment that may or may not resonate with exactly what you're looking for in a podcast microphone.

Chapter 10
Podcast Student Stories -"Idea to iTunes" Success Stories

Now that I've shown you almost everything you need to know about starting a podcast, I'd like to share with you a few success stories from my students who have gone "from idea to iTunes," and launched a podcast with my PodcastLaunchLab. com program.

This chapter is all about the students who I've helped start a podcast. They all started out the same way, with a story to tell. That is what a podcast does, it gives you a platform to tell your story. To share your experience, to help others.

It is my hope that these stories encourage you to do the same.

Caroline Gardner - Host of the "Why We Tri" Podcast

I met Caroline through a mutual friend at the gym. When we talk alignment, that is exactly what took place on our first call. Caroline was extremely clear on the podcasting path that she wanted to take with her show. She shared with me that not so long ago, she viewed triathlons as something she would NEVER do, that was; until she did.

She felt VERY strong about sharing her story of perseverance with the world, and that is exactly what she's done, and I couldn't be more proud of her!

Have you ever looked at a triathlon and thought, "that's crazy!" I had thought the same thing until about five years ago when I set out on a mission to "tri" and do things I NEVER thought I could!

In October of 2018, my 75-year-old, independent Mother, Kathleen K. Gardener of Unionville, Connecticut, lost her fight against an infection in just under 10 days of entering the hospital. Today, I realize I was fortunate to be by her side during her last days. Upon returning to Miami, there were days I could not get out of bed and attend to my three daughters, who were in great need of their Mom. My WHY was deflated.

Finding self-motivation when the world beneath you is crumbling seems impossible. In triathlon, you must be in the present moment at all times. One second of losing focus and you could be underwater, flown off your bike, or trip and fall.

My three daughters needed their Mom back, and I needed my WHY back. Small attempts back into the pool to swim, on the bike to cycle, and out on the track to run, I was surrounded by a WORLD of triathletes through Iron Man, who all shared their incredible stories with me. These stories inspire me to get back up, keep going, and SHARE, but I wasn't done there, I knew if I had conquered triathlons, I could conquer a podcast, and that's exactly what I did, thanks to the help of Sebastian and the PodcastLaunchLab.com!

Ozzie Martinez, Jr. - Host of the "Post Traumatic Survival Podcast"

I never really know where a new student may show up. I met Ozzie through an old high school friend. He mentioned that Ozzie was starting a podcast and he may need some help, even though he pretty much had everything lined up to launch.

Ozzie and I had a quick call, and he decided that he needed to hire me for a month to help him close up some loose ends and get the show launched.

We worked on creating this show name, the album art, and the intro and outro for the show. Ozzie is a very take charge kind of guy, so he took everything I told him to do and ran with it, X10. I always love when this happens. I get to share in the excitement with my students as they embark on their podcasting journey.

Here's Ozzie's story...

Osvaldo "Ozzie" Martinez Jr served in the United States Marine Corps from 2002-2006.

In February of 2004, he deployed to Fallujah, Iraq with the 3rd AABN (Assault Amphibian Battalion) Alpha Company, where they experienced heavy combat, and his unit lost five Marines. He deployed again in 2005 on the 13 MEU (Marine Expeditionary Unit) attached to 2/1. There, his unit took six casualties, including their commanding officer, Major Ray Mendoza.

Ozzie got out of the Corps in 2006, moved back to Miami, and thought he was done with the Marines, until he received reactivation orders from the inactive reserves in 2008. That's when his severe PTSD symptoms started to reveal themselves. He started going to the VA, and shortly after was rated 70% disabled for PTSD. Eventually, the Marines would send him a letter that due to PTSD, he was non-deployable, so he never left.

But his PTSD never left either. In 2010, he met his wife. He was having a hard time with keeping a job and was really struggling. The VA reevaluated him and raised his service-connected rating to 100% P&T (permanent and total). In January of 2011, Ozzie and his wife got married. In May of that year, Ozzie found out a friend that he had deployed with twice had taken his own life.

Ozzie started to drink heavily, and obviously that didn't mix well with his meds. His son was born in July, and although his birth brought happiness to his life, he was still drinking hard. In early 2012, Ozzie and his wife separated but never divorced. He was living alone and had totally hit rock bottom! He isolated himself from pretty much everyone he knew. His turning point came in September of 2014. A few of the Marines from Alpha Company decided to have a reunion to mark the 10 years since Fallujah.

All of them had been friends on social media, but they never spoke about the negative stuff in their lives, so he felt like he was going through PTSD alone. However, talking with each other, he realized he wasn't alone. A lot of the Marines there were going through the same things. He came back from that reunion different. He knew he wasn't alone. Shortly after, Ozzie and his wife started working things out and got back together. Ozzie felt like he had to find a way to help fellow combat veterans with PTSD to know that they weren't alone. So, in June 2015, he started a small nonprofit in Miami, Florida, called Operation WetVet (www.operationwetvet.org). After a few years, Ozzie decided to study psychology full-time with hopes to better understand PTSD. In 2020, he decided to start a podcast called The Post Traumatic Survival Podcast.

As you can see, Ozzie has quite the story! Which is exactly why he was so eager to start his podcast. He didn't just start a podcast for himself, he did it for other people. Other people with similar or even worse stories than his. Ozzie's goal is to impact people through his story and to help them rebound like he did.

It was nothing short of a privilege to work with Ozzie, and we're still in touch as he keeps me posted on how the show is going.

I appreciate you, Ozzie!

Barbie Winterbottom - Business of HR Podcast

Barbie found me via my YouTube channel. She had been searching for tips and tricks on getting her podcast started. While she did make some progress, she could only get so far.

Barbie is a great example of the "go-getter" clients that I come in contact with. She had a thorough understanding of the basics of what she needed, but when it came to figuring out her equipment set up and a few other loose ends that needed to be done before launching, she knew that she needed to hire an expert, and that is exactly what she did.

Here's Barbie's story in her own words...

After I left the office on May 14, 2020, I called my wife from the car to let her know I had just lost my job. I was informed at 10am by my boss that as a result of COVID-19 and its impact on the business that my position as Chief Human Resource Officer had been eliminated.

I drove home and immediately started thinking about my next steps. Knowing the organization I worked for was owned by a private equity firm, I assumed that in 3 to 5 years, the company would sell and I would be impacted, so I had loosely laid out some ideas and plans to launch my own company. Those plans just got fast forwarded in an instant.

It was time to bring my plans to life. I had been actively building my following and influence on LinkedIn with content including videos and blogs. My goal was to create several social channels all feeding into an online community built to nurture and grow HR talent.

I was fortunate to have been a guest on many podcasts and webinars and been gathering advice from some incredibly seasoned and talented folks who were also generous and willing to help me get started.

I was doing pretty well on creating my videos, my blog, and my following was growing exponentially, I knew the next step was to launch my podcast.

I was given a list of all the best equipment to produce the podcast, and I was off and running. I placed my order, and since it was in the midst of Covid, and apparently half the world was podcasting, my equipment took weeks to come in. While I was waiting for my equipment, I read everything I could on podcasting. I purchased an online course for $99 and figured I would be good to go.

Then my equipment came in, one piece at a time, and I was incredibly excited to get started. I unboxed my equipment, hooked up all the cords (lots of cords), and was ready to go.

Here's where the problems started. Nowhere in the online course, the equipment list I had been given, or my reading and research did anyone tell me exactly how to use the ACTUAL equipment. I was at a loss. I searched, went to the product websites, used Google and YouTube for weeks, and - nothing. I was at a point of frustration beyond anything I had felt before, as something so simple was stumping me. I had downloaded multiple soft-ware tools to no avail, and then, after exhausting all avenues, I decided to search YouTube one last time and change the search string a bit... and that's when it happened.

I changed the search string, and one video popped up, crazy now that I think about it, for only one video to pop up, but there it was. I clicked on it, and the energy and authenticity jumped out of my computer and I immediately knew I needed to talk to this person. I looked up his name and company, sent a chat through his website, and called him immediately! I was thrilled to receive a response within 15 minutes, and Sebastian and I talked for the first time.

In the first two minutes of the call, I knew that I had found the person who could help me bring my podcast to life. Thank you, Sebastian, you rock!

Lynn A. Howard - Confessions of a Digital Nomad

I met Lynn back in 2005 at a BNI International Conference in Long Beach, California. We kept in touch via Facebook for years after that, and in early 2020, she reached out and said she was ready to start her podcast.

She is currently a digital nomad. She travels the world and lives in places that she loves. At the time of this writing, she is in Bangkok, Thailand. Talk about livin' the dream!

Based on her nomadic lifestyle, I thought it was a no-brainer to name her show "Confessions of a Digital Nomad" - and so we did!

Lynn is a speaker, author, and coach who is on a mission to help people live their best life.

Here's Lynn's story of starting a podcast.

Why did I start this podcast?

My coaching clients often tell me that they hear my voice in their head. Now it's about to be a real thing. Just kidding (sort of).

The truth is, COVID made me do it. All sorts of people, from strangers I've met at airport bars to audience members at speaking events, clients, and friends have been telling me for YEARS that I need to do a podcast. It turns out that the world turning upside down was what it took for the perfectionist in me to jump. (Ha!)

Staying in Bangkok, Thailand, where I've spent the last five months of quarantine, has made me crave connection more than ever. It's also given me time to reflect on all the life-changing connections that I have made. I feel so much gratitude for them – including you, reading this blog post right now.

I've had the privilege to meet and connect with so many amazing individuals at conferences and speaking events that I've attended around the world in the last 10 + years. "People and possibilities" – being a connector and supporter of people – is my passion. My mission while on this planet is to inspire, uplift, and help my fellow soul-filled humans trekking along on their own journey of life to align with their true greatness, just as others have helped me.

Those of you who know me, you know my journey hasn't been an easy one. From the time I was born, I've survived and persevered. I've raised children as a single mom, started and sold businesses, and served in major leadership roles across the globe. In 2019, I started a new chapter in my life as a digital nomad.

On the road, this podcast is also a way for me to stay rooted. It's like a home of sorts, a gathering place — somewhere for entrepreneurs and growth-minded people to come to get inspired, make connections, and feed their mind and spirit.

Shay Rowbottom - Host of "The Shay Rowbottom Show"

How I found Shay is probably one of the most interesting stories to date.

I had been following Shay on LinkedIn for about a year, and I really enjoyed her content. She's funny, entertaining, and informative. Not to mention the fact that she is absolutely CRUSHING the LinkedIn content and follower game.

#ProTip: if you don't follow Shay on LinkedIn, you totally should: https://www.linkedin.com/in/shayrowbottom/

I had reached out to Shay and her team a few different times but was unsuccessful booking her on the show. Then one day

I was meeting with one of my other students who was currently launching a podcast. He's a coach and told me that he had been working with a local "LinkedIn Influencer" - jokingly I asked him, "Is her name Shay?" -to which his eyes opened large and he paused and said, "Yes, yes it is!"

At that moment, I knew that I was one step closer to connecting with Shay and getting her on my podcast.

Two days later, I got a calendar request from Shay and it was GAME ON!

I was just about to open my new podcast studio, so that timing was perfect, as I wanted Shay to be the first podcast guest in the new studio.

When we were done with the interview, I quickly asked Shay, "So, when are you starting a podcast?" She said, "it's definitely something to consider," and the conversation kind of fell by the wayside. Then three months later, she called me and said "I want to start a podcast, and I want to hire you to help me make it happen. I have a story to tell about my traumatic childhood and how I was able to heal from it, and I want to help other people do the same. That's why I want to start a podcast."

She immediately had my interest as she was explicitly clear on her WHY!

Her show has been a success out of the gates with close to 5,000 downloads on the first day!

Now I do want to mention that Shay's out of the gates success was due to her having a GIANT following on LinkedIn and has built quite the community around her, so launching a podcast was a bit easier than the average person just starting. The rest is history.

Here's Shay's story.

I wanted to kill myself. I thought about suicide on a weekly basis for years. I was depressed, addicted, co-dependent, and on my last hope. I took a chance on an alternative healing modality to give one final go at self-recovery before deciding to end it all. What I found on the other side was nothing short of a miracle. My life changed... forever. I've never been the same, and I've never looked back. I recovered my independence, my soul, my freedom. And now, I'm here to help others do the same. This is the story of how I became broken, and how I put myself back together again. Buckle up. www.shayrowbottom.com/

Shortly before launching her podcast, she launched a new company called "Heal Tribe" which is designed to help people work through past trauma by means of coaching, community, and support. You can find out more about that at: Shayrowbottom.com/healtribe

As you've read, these are all incredible stories of people who have made the decision to launch a podcast and serve the world in some capacity or another. I'm here to tell you today that you can do the same thing. You have the same unique ability as everyone I've mentioned above, you just need to DO IT!

The time is NOW!

Chapter 11
ANYTHING is Possible,
But Only 100% of the Time

YES, YOU CAN!

Maybe you've heard this before, but I'm gonna go ahead and tell you again: yes, you can! I know it may sound very cheesy and cliché, but a lot of people don't follow their dreams, or they never have been given permission to follow their dreams and do what they want! I'm giving you permission right now, permission to follow your dreams, permission to launch that podcast, permission to tell your story, permission to just do it!

When I first heard that phrase, my ego automatically kicked in. I was like, I can? Of course I can -- I know that I can. But I sat there for a moment and considered that phrase. I remember how many times I've heard in my life that I couldn't do it. By friends, colleagues, family -- you name it. When your ideas are crazy enough, some people will never buy in. That's their problem.

If you constantly stay focused on what other people's thought process is and what their opinions are, you'll never get anywhere. You have to believe in yourself. You have to believe you can do it. You have to give yourself permission to do it. I firmly believe that if you don't believe in yourself, no one else is going to. If you don't give yourself permission, no one else will. So, why not grant yourself that one wish right now and tell yourself, yes, yes I can.

I don't care if you have to stand in front of a mirror. I don't care if you have to stand on top of your bed and scream at the top of your lungs, give yourself permission to follow through with what you know you want to do.

You Have to Believe it!

You not only have to see it, you have to believe it, you have to believe in yourself, believe in your podcast, believe in the people you connect with, believe that it's actually possible. If you don't believe it, no one else will.

Don't worry about the naysayers, doubters, and just plain negative people who are negative by nature. You're never going to change their perspective or their mind on what you know is right for you.

What would next year look like if you started your podcast right now?

What would the next five years look like if you started your podcast right now?

What would your future look like if you started your podcast right now?

These are critical questions to ask yourself when taking on a task like launching a podcast.

Podcasts aren't for everyone. I have mentioned that several times in this book, but a podcast is clearly for you because of your vision. So, I strongly encourage you to dig deep and put together a plan that allows you to execute starting a podcast right now, not tomorrow, not next week, not next month, not next year, right now!

I would like to tell you that if you start a podcast right now, this time next year - you're going to be so stoked that you did. Make a decision that you're going to make you do something right now and evaluate how it went this time next year.

I always like to look at the things that I didn't procrastinate on and I didn't delay on, and I look back and say, "I'm glad I started when I did!"

Podcasting is one of those things. When I started my brand in 2010, I wanted a podcast because I wanted to "radio on the internet" and a podcast was the best way to do that. I saw the vision in my mind where the podcast was now and where it was going to be.

I saw the transition of where radio was and where it's headed (which is out the door by the way). Radio may never completely disappear, but I firmly believe that technology like satellite radio and podcasting will supersede anything that remains in the radio world as we know it.

I can't remember the last time I turned on the FM radio in my car. I am a satellite radio subscriber to SiriusXM, and I absolutely love it. I love it just as much as I love podcasting. They both have commercials and ads within the content, but they're digestible, relevant, and sometimes I actually learn something (who would've known that you can order a tuxedo from an app on your phone and have it delivered to your door and have it fit you perfectly??).

What else is possible by starting a podcast?

So we just got done talking about what a year from now would look like, five years would look like, your future would look like if you started your podcast right now, if you decide to take action right now. But I also ask you what else is possible... but you are starting a podcast, right, and I am a firm believer that anything is possible, but only 100% of the time.

What Would a Podcast do For Your Life Overall?

Many times, I've had students go through the program at the PodcastLaunchLab.com and find that their podcast not only became an extension of their brand, but also became a hobby in their life, something that they thoroughly enjoy doing. Sometimes the podcast was started out of pure leisure and turned into a business. But when you look at starting a podcast as part of what it's going to do for your life overall, there are several different things that can happen. The goal is to stay OPEN to whatever comes your way.

What Would a Podcast do for Your Business?

I talked to an extent throughout this book about what a podcast will do for you and your brand, and it's a no-brainer that having a podcast gives you an advantage as a business, especially if your competition doesn't have a podcast and has no plans in the near future of starting one. This gives you an opportunity to reach people that you aren't currently reaching in the audio space. People listen to podcasts, and those people may very well want to do business with you.

What Would a Podcast do for Your Local Community?

A great way to work with your local community is to be able to help people in it gain exposure through your podcast. You can do remote recordings, interviewing small business owners, people who are in your community who own small businesses. Another great idea would be to approach these small businesses and help them understand what you can do to bring exposure to them through your podcast. Local communities are obviously limited pertaining to your podcast, but it's a phenomenal opportunity for you to be able to contribute and support your local community.

What would a podcast do for your mission?

In my opinion, there are endless opportunities to start a podcast. I mentioned a lot of them in this book: developing relationships, growing your business and brand, to being able to impact people's lives for the better by shifting their mindset based on something heard on a podcast.

All of us have different experiences and different opportunities that show up in our lives, so I'm not here to tell you exactly what's possible. I'm simply sharing my experience, as well as what I believe are the possibilities within the space of podcasting.

I started to go all in with podcasting at the end of 2016, so I've been at this for roughly four years now. In those four years, I have heard more negative feedback and push back from those closest to me and those in my community than I ever have before. I've chosen to put the blinders on, ignore the noise, and stay the course. When you know you're racing on the right track, you know. You feel it in your gut and feel overwhelmed with certainty. When things like that happen, they are not to be ignored. There's a direct instruction from your human instinct on where you should be and what you should be doing.

So, when you're considering what's possible, it's wise to stay away from negative people, naysayers, and people who think that what you think is possible actually is not. Chances are; those are people who've never built anything worthwhile. Stay away from them!

What Kind of Impact can You Make with Your Podcast?

A good question to ask yourself before you set out on this venture is "What kind of impact do I expect to make with my podcast?"

Even if you don't know what kind of impact you want to make with your podcast, dream a little bit, use your imagination a little bit, act as if it's already real for a minute. Envision what is possible from starting a podcast and the impact it can make in the world. Again, whatever you have to do, make it up, dream it up, think it up, daydream it up. Do whatever you've got to do to visualize the possible impacts your podcast can make.

How are You Hoping to Change People's Lives?

You may not know the answer to this question when you start your podcast, and that's completely okay. I had no idea that I was going to change people's lives by empowering and encouraging them to tell their story through a rigorously honest process of starting a podcast. But I did, and people's lives are being changed, including mine.

More times than not, we can't predict the way things are going to happen they just happen when they're supposed to happen. I wouldn't change any of it. Knowing I'm doing work that matters and impacting others is enough for me. There is no boredom when things are like that.

How do you want to impact others?

Yes, these questions are all forms of asking yourself how you're going to serve your fellow human. I believe doing work that matters is the most important thing we can do in this life. Just having a podcast to have a podcast makes zero sense. Having a podcast to give back to the world and make it a better place makes a ton of sense.

The reason I'm bringing all this up at the end of this book is that I want to empower and encourage you to really dig deep and think deep about what your overall strategy is pertaining to making an impact with your podcast. We all want to do work that matters. In my opinion, having a podcast that serves others is doing work that matters. Only you know what you're passionate about and no one can tell you that. So when you're putting your plan together to launch a show and you decide what you're going to talk about, what the shows are going to be about, I strongly encourage and challenge you to consider these factors.

Focus on Doing Work that Matters.

I think it goes without saying that when you do work that matters, it gives you a level of fulfillment. First of all, you know that you're doing something to make an impact in someone's life, which in turn makes the world a better place.

Never in a million years did I think that getting into the podcasting world would mean doing work that matters. I mean, to a certain extent, it mattered because I was helping people do something they could probably do themselves, just because they didn't know how to. I continue to attract and meet new individuals with extremely interesting stories that they feel compelled to tell via a podcast: all kinds of stories from rags to riches and back to rags, traumatic childhoods, a marriage didn't work out, people who have come back from war different and almost unable recover but did. I could go on and on.

I can truly say there's nothing better than doing work that matters.

Focus on Work that Serves Others

The best way to do work that matters is to focus on doing work that serves other people. When you're in service to other people, you automatically take the focus off yourself. Which is the way it should be. Earlier in the book, I talked about how to interview people, and the number one tip I gave you is making sure that it is all about them, or at least mostly about them. I referenced what the great Larry King once said about making an interview 80/20. Eighty percent about your guest and 20% about you asking the questions and replying to your guests.

Yes, interviewing someone is a form of serving them and their brand for the world.

Focus on building a legacy that will outlive you.

These are all great ways to ensure that you make an impact on what you're doing pertaining to the start of your podcast and making it a part of your business.

I APPRECIATE YOU AND BELIEVE IN YOU!

Well, friends, this is where the journey of this book starts to close. All this means is that the beginning of your podcast journey is about to start, or maybe it's even started because you couldn't wait to get done with the book. That's exciting just to think about!

I want to thank you for taking time out of your life to read this book. I appreciate it more than you can ever know. I wrote this book because it's on mission with my brand, which is to help people tell their story by starting a podcast. I truly believe that podcasters are going to change the world. Story changes the world. People change the world. I think podcast-ing is where all of those worlds collide at once.

That really is a beautiful thing. It is my hope that you take all the tools and resources that you've learned reading this book and implement them right away! Don't delay, don't wait until tomorrow, don't wait until next week, don't wait until you leave your job. Start today! You'll thank me for doing so. I think I've covered enough about procrastination in this book so I won't go into it as I close things out.

But I will remind you that you are the only thing in the way of you and your microphone and recording a new podcast episode. The world is waiting to hear your story. You never know who's going to be listening or who is going to be impacted by your show, and that's why I'm doing it. It's just that important.

I believe in you because you believe in me. That's obvious because you're reading this book.

Now it's time to saddle up, get focused, get out of your own way, shrug procrastination off, and launch that podcast.

If you've read this book and you're ready to launch your podcast, but feel that hiring an expert to help you through the process may be a better option for you, you can schedule a FREE Strategy Call with myself or someone on the launch team here:

PodcastLaunchLabNow.com

www.ingramcontent.com/pod-product-compliance
Lightning Source LLC
Chambersburg PA
CBHW070959050326
40689CB00014B/3412